Alasdair Sutherland was born in Glasgow, only child of William, a design engineer, and housewife, Janet. After education at Lenzie Primary, Lenzie Academy and Glasgow University, he won a place at the College at Hamble where British Airways trained their pilots. His career progressed from HS Tridents, L1011, to twin turboprops where he achieved command. Then, after a couple of years as senior copilot on the B747-400, it was back to the left seat on B757/767. The 9/11 attack had a big impact. After compulsory retirement, interest in aviation continued but he concentrated on designing and flying model aircraft.

I was twenty-four before I started a proper paid job, and so I owe my parents a great deal for supporting me for so long. And my wife has tolerated me amazingly well for a very long time. Our two daughters were remarkably well-behaved and gave us not a moment's anguish, and now it is comforting to see them settled, with great husbands and adorable children. So what can go wrong? Well, you could put this book back on the shelf and select one by someone with a more troubled past. Or you could make my day by buying it to read about all the little incidents that even my family members don't know about yet.

Alasdair Sutherland

A Pilot's Ups and Downs

Memoirs of a British Airline Pilot

Austin Macauley Publishers

LONDON * CAMBRIDGE * NEW YORK * SHARJAH

Copyright © Alasdair Sutherland 2024

The right of Alasdair Sutherland to be identified as author of this work has been asserted by the author in accordance with sections 77 and 78 of the Copyright, Designs and Patents Act 1988.

All rights reserved. No part of this publication may be reproduced, stored in a retrieval system, or transmitted in any form or by any means, electronic, mechanical, photocopying, recording, or otherwise, without the prior permission of the publishers.

Any person who commits any unauthorised act in relation to this publication may be liable to criminal prosecution and civil claims for damages.

All of the events in this memoir are true to the best of author's memory. The views expressed in this memoir are solely those of the author.

A CIP catalogue record for this title is available from the British Library.

ISBN 9781035819782 (Paperback)
ISBN 9781035819799 (ePub e-book)

www.austinmacauley.com

First Published 2024
Austin Macauley Publishers Ltd®
1 Canada Square
Canary Wharf
London
E14 5AA

Table of Contents

Prologue	9
Chapter 1: My Background	11
Chapter 2: College of Air Training, Hamble	26
Chapter 3: Aviation in General CAA Rules	37
Chapter 4: Joining BEA	47
Chapter 5: Flying the Cabin	70
Chapter 6: TriStar	93
Chapter 7: Twin Turboprops	110
Chapter 8: Longhaul on the 747	133
Chapter 9: Jet Command	151
Chapter 10: After 9/11	168
Chapter 11: And This Is Now	179
Chapter 12: Aircraft Designer	186
Glossary	191

Prologue

People have often said to me, "Oh, you must have seen some changes in aviation over all those years!" and after a little thought, I'd reply, "No!"

I had missed the fundamental changes, the biplanes replaced by monoplanes, wood and fabric replaced by aluminium alloys, piston engines replaced by turbines, navigators, radio operators and flight engineers replaced by electronics. In 1974 the first airliner I flew was very fast, smooth and comfortable. It could operate in all weather, fly above the clouds in clear air, land at any major airport and the autopilot could do everything but take off.

The Trident pioneered automatic 'blind' landings in bad visibility which is still not universally available. It was very noisy, measured under the take-off path, but in the cockpit it was quiet and comfortable. My last aeroplane, the Boeing 767 could do all those same things, was almost as fast, and much more efficient. The latest airliners have even more automated electronics, and slightly better fuel economy.

Flying is a bit safer than it was, with electronic safety gizmos and super-reliable engines and systems, but there is still no reset or 'back' button as in computer games for when the pilot gets it wrong. The old saying goes that there are old pilots, and bold pilots, but there are no old bold pilots. I got to be an old pilot.

I have to admit though, it is quite a boring job on the whole. In fact that is what the job is all about, making the flight as boring as possible for the passengers by foreseeing and circumventing any possible source of danger or excitement. We want the passengers to tell their friends about the meal and in-flight movie. So boring is good, a success. Makes you wonder why I wrote about it then. I suppose people might be interested in how I got into the job in the first place, especially if they harbour ambitions for a career in aviation.

You might be interested in how we go about learning to operate in an environment that to the layman is a labyrinth of dials, knobs and switches. Travel books are always popular, and this book is as much about travel as flying. Plus, I can throw in a bunch of anecdotes about the more exciting times I had, or heard about, during my 31-year career.

I have changed the names of most of the other people involved in the narrative to avoid any chance of causing offence, except for close friends or instances where no offence could be taken.

Chapter 1
My Background

I was part of the Baby Boomer generation, born very early in the nineteen fifties in the east end of Glasgow. My first home had two rooms, and no toilet. The toilet was off the communal staircase of the tenement block. Of course I have no memories of that, as I was two and a half when we moved to a spacious terraced house with a garden, in a leafy suburb, more befitting the family of an enthusiastic and ambitious engineer. My father worked for the King Aircraft Corporation which sounds very grand, as it was meant to. Mr King had great ambitions for his little engineering company in Glasgow, and put great effort into investing in all the latest tools and equipment and hiring the best staff. I grew up knowing that virtually all British civil and military aircraft of the day had bits and pieces made by King Aircraft and designed (in part) by my dad.

They sold pipe clamps, flexible hoses with self-sealing couplings for fluids and hot gas, cowling fasteners, seat mechanisms, and so on. I have an early memory of seeing a large box containing some kind of mechanism for a Bristol Britannia in the house, on its way to an Airshow. My dad worked on the King Aircraft trade stand at the Farnborough and Paris Airshows every year, and each year he came home with a toy, or model aircraft. I was too young to build and paint Airfix kits myself, but I watched with great interest as my father made a splendid job of building and painting them for me.

I had all the usual toys, clockwork model boats, an electric model train, lots of model cars and trucks (Dinky was the leading brand I remember), and later an electric model slot-car track, one of the cars being an Austin A40 Farina, the latest groundbreaking design by the fashionable Italian designer. One distinct memory of childhood is of a toy aeroplane, a Gloster Javelin, that when pushed along the floor was kept going by the flywheel motor. When it encountered a piece of furniture or skirting board a little red button on the nose was pushed in, and out popped the pilot in his ejector seat.

At the age of four and a half I started school in Lenzie Primary, and was thus the youngest in the class, all through primary school. It was an old building, and badly overcrowded. When I was in year 2 I remember that I was in one of two classes in the church hall across the road from the school. I was not too keen on school but learned to get by, and my pushy mother helped me get through the lessons by making sure I learned my spelling words and times tables, and she set me a little extra homework besides. She also sent me to private elocution lessons, in order to smooth off my Glasgow accent, that was deeply unfashionable for many years, until Stanley Baxter invented "Parliamo Glasgow" and Billy Connolly appeared on Parkinson's chat show.

By my sixth or seventh year of school, the big old, overcrowded building that used to house both Primary and Secondary had many empty rooms, and a chilled hollow echo to the place, after a brand-new Secondary school had been built. My primary 7 class even had a room set aside for our "project building" (I used twigs and ice-lolly sticks to model a sawmill). In my time we sat an examination in primary 7 called the 11-plus, that set us on the career path determined by the results. The best, A grade, pupils were rewarded with a "two language course" in senior school, and were destined for school certificates followed by higher education. The next batch (B grade) were assessed suitable for a one language course, while those deemed unsuitable to learn another language (C grade) were expected to leave school early for training in a practical job.

All through school I remember being quite socially backward, discomfited at being the weakest and slowest in PE, and embarrassed by the country dancing lessons I endured as part of the PE curriculum. However I do remember that, somehow or other, I had a date for our primary 7, final year graduation dance. Sylvia was my partner for the evening, she was pretty and polite and we had a lovely evening. I don't think I saw her again, as I have no memory of her at Secondary School.

At about this time my parents bought their first car which was used for visiting relatives, sightseeing and for hill-walking expeditions around Scotland. On these trips, which varied from day-trips to two-week annual holidays, I would sit in the back with a whole pile of maps, looking out all around and map-reading my way along the route. My father had taught me to map-read, and most of the maps I used were the one inch to the mile Ordnance Survey maps which were very detailed and allowed our progress to be checked against all sorts of natural and man-made features. These maps were useful on the hills too. This skill was a great help in school geography and essential in visual navigation when learning to fly.

Lenzie Academy was considered a good school, and the teaching standards were high, in maths, science, Latin and modern languages at least (English, not so much). I was one of the ones selected to learn French and Latin among all the other usual subjects, but I had only just made the cut as I was in the third "A" class. However after the first term I was moved up to the top A class, along with Wilma from Auchinloch and 4 others. I was still the youngest in the year, but did reasonably well especially in Maths & Science, but not English and history which I hated.

I mentioned Wilma in particular as all through school we were in the same class and by fourth year I was smitten. I gazed at her in class and took every opportunity to meet her by chance for a brief casual conversation, but I knew she was out of my league socially. I was the shy awkward geek; she was in the school hockey team, a singer in the annual school Gilbert & Sullivan opera production and she played a leading role, Lydia, in the school drama club's production of Sheridan's play "The Rivals."

Because of her I joined the club and helped move the props on stage, and I still have the annotated script and the programme with Wilma's name at the top and mine in small print at the bottom. Even in first year at University I would meet her on the bus home sometimes and sit beside her, or ask her to sit with me. I don't know what tales of woe she may have told her friends, but to me she was always very polite, charming and kind, and chatted away in a friendly manner, for which I have always been grateful as it gradually helped me overcome my shyness and under-confidence.

I used to daydream that one day when I was a dashing young airline pilot we would meet again and after a whirlwind romance we'd get married. Wilma was my first love, totally one-sided, but I still remember her fondly.

My links with aviation and engineering continued all through my school days. I was taken abroad on holiday, unusual in those days, at the ages of six, nine and twelve, and the smell of the kerosene-burning Viscounts, Vanguards and the Comet jet was the essence of romantic air travel, enjoyed by the select few. My father was in charge of King Aircraft's drawing office, and one of the many subcontract jobs they did was some detail design work on a new British three-engined airliner, the de Havilland (later Hawker Siddeley) Trident, named after Neptune's three-pointed spear.

I heard all about the Trident, the world's first trijet, and how advanced it was going to be. During my later years at school my father got me a Saturday job at the new Glasgow airport washing aeroplanes for Loganair, a fledgling operator that had just been awarded the contract for the air ambulance in Scotland, using the new BN Islander aircraft fitted with stretchers designed and built by King Aircraft. Loganair was the lead operator of the Islander and their chief pilot, Duncan MacIntosh, flew the demonstrator at the 1966 Farnborough Airshow. I was taken to the show at Farnborough that year as a special treat and met several engineers and pilots.

Good results in Physics, Chemistry, Maths and French and a barely scraped pass in English earned me acceptances for University places in Scotland, and I went for Glasgow as my first choice as they offered Aeronautical Engineering. I had every intention at this stage of seeking a career as an airline pilot, but various people had advised that, as a plan B, I should get a university degree first since piloting was a chancy career. A neighbour of an uncle had trained as a pilot and joined BEA, but left after a few years. I often wondered why.

When enrolling for my first year at Glasgow University I told the lady at the desk my name and course, she ticked me off the list and wrote my name on the Matriculation card. She handed me the card and dismissed me with a slight gesture, however I paused and objected, "You filled in my name as Alexander instead of Alasdair!"

She gave a smile and explained condescendingly, "We always use the Latin equivalent names where possible."

I enrolled in the Aeronautical Engineering course at Glasgow, the only Scottish establishment to offer an Aero option. I had been accepted for Engineering at other places, including Strathclyde University in Glasgow, one of a number of prestigious Colleges which had been granted full University status a few years previously. My father had done his engineering training there, when it was 'The Tech,' more formally the Royal College of Science and Technology, but most Glasgow students still called it The Tech, especially those of us with Latin names. The University Air Squadron had a promotional display in the Matric hall. I headed over and said, "Gaun'ae gie us, I mean, please may I have an application form?"

In the first-year engineering class there were more than two hundred of us, all male. There was not a single female student in Engineering that year. There were however a few students younger than me, since they had come straight from fifth year at school. Some had to wait a year before they were legally allowed into the bar in the Men's Union, our social club where we had lunch and socialised. Yes, even here we were segregated. The women had their own Union, where men were not allowed except for dances and other social events. However in first year I did sometimes sit with Wilma on the bus home, the highlight of my week, but I've never seen her since.

From 9 until 1 we had lectures and tutorials every day and then, after an hour for lunch, laboratory work 2-5 p.m. every afternoon except Wednesday. Subjects were physics, chemistry, mathematics, mechanics and engineering drawing. The free afternoons on Wednesdays were meant to be used for sporting activity. I tried playing squash several times, and visited the swimming pool and sauna, but more often went to the cinema. I was really pleased when I scored 98% in a Mechanics exam in first year, first equal with one of the golden boys who excelled at everything, and had skipped sixth year at school making him one of the few younger than me. I was bitterly disappointed however to fail the mathematics exam at the end of first year, necessitating an autumn re-sit which rather took the gloss off my amazing summer.

University Air Squadron

Having heard nothing since the medical and interviews in October, I was pleasantly surprised, shortly after the second term began (and my eighteenth birthday), to receive an invitation to join the Air Squadron. The squadron then was all male, like the rest of my life, except for Miss Sinclair the secretary who was a middle-aged spinster (to an eighteen-year-old) and a lovely person.

The deal, and you too might find this hard to believe, was that they would lay on aviation related lectures every Thursday evening in the posh city centre headquarters in Park Circus, followed by a beer in the subsidised bar, and at weekends (not every weekend, we took turns) they drove us to Scone, a grass airfield near Perth where the Chipmunks were based. There we stayed Friday and Saturday nights in the squadron cottages, two or three to a room, attended briefings in the operations room, and were taught to fly Chipmunks by experienced RAF instructors.

They also had a subsidised bar for informal debriefing sessions in the evening. Then they ***paid*** us over a pound a day, plus five bob (now called 25 pence) for attending evening lectures, which covered our bar expenses (told you it was cheap).

The rough cadet-pilot uniform plus the beautifully made flying suit, white kid-leather gloves and bone-dome helmet were all supplied, and each time we flew we were issued with a parachute which we checked, and strapped on tightly before walking out to the aeroplane (with the gait of a chimpanzee, the straps were so tight). The parachute pack itself dangled under one's bottom and formed the seat cushion.

De Havilland's first Canadian design, and intended as a successor to the Tiger Moth biplane trainer of WW2, the DHC1 Chipmunk was an all-metal, low wing, single-engined, two-seat aircraft with its main wheels on struts at the front of the wing, and a tailwheel. The student sat in the front seat, with the instructor in the rear. Though the structure was all metal, the control surfaces and the wing aft of the spar were fabric-covered, just like the whole of the Tiger Moth.

The Gypsy Major engine used in the later Tiger Moths was used again in the Chipmunk, giving it a top speed almost 30 mph faster than the draggy biplane. The metal-framed canopy glazed with Perspex covered both cockpits, gave a great view all-round and slid to the rear for access. The Chipmunks we used were British built, but others were built in Canada and Portugal.

The Chipmunk had a 'fighter' joystick, used right-handed, rudder pedals, a throttle and mixture control on the left sidewall, and it was a joy to fly. The controls were light and harmonious. Instruments were basic but we flew visually anyway. The flaps were manually operated by a big lever on the right side with three positions, up, take-off and land. The only slightly tricky aspect to operating the Chipmunk was the braking system. A lever could be pulled back to apply the wheel brakes, but we used them only for parking and taxying. As with any taildragger, if you brake sharply while trundling forward the aircraft could tip on its nose.

The brake was pulled fully on only for parking, but when we started to taxi we put the brake right off, applied full rudder either way, then pulled the brake lever back until it started to bite, and locked it in that position. The result was that deflecting the rudder left or right gave progressive differential braking on the left or right wheel. That allowed us to steer, as the tailwheel was free to castor, not connected to the rudder control in any way.

The brake lever stayed in that position for the whole flight because on landing, with no prop wash over the rudder, differential braking was our only means of steering on the landing roll. When coming to a complete stop, especially on tarmac, very gentle use of the brake lever was needed to stop without lifting the tail. I never had a problem with setting the brake for taxying but some pilots hated it.

On my first evening at the Squadron HQ there was an informal get-together in civilian dress, an opportunity for the newly joined students to meet each other and the flying instructors, all RAF Officers. I circulated round the room, with the usual opening line, "What are you studying?" and I was just about to ask this to a fresh-faced young chap when one of the senior cadets broke in with, "I'd like to introduce you to Flight Lieutenant Brooke, the Squadron Adjutant."

Flt. Lt. (or Mike) Brooke was a very friendly chap, with a very young face and a host of funny stories. He related that when he joined the RAF his first preference was to be a navigator, but during his Officer Training Course he was offered the opportunity to switch to pilot training, with the promise that if he dropped out he would revert to navigator training. Well he didn't drop out, however during a medical examination just after receiving his wings, the doctor had some grave news, "You are under the minimum height to be a pilot!" There was a minimum height stipulated in regulations, and various aircraft had their own maximum height limits as well (often related to ejecting in one piece).

However, the wing commander in charge of that stage of his flying training decreed that the RAF had spent too much on Mike's training to put him back three years, so he remained a pilot and went on to fly for the RAF for nearly 35 years![1]

There was a corollary to that story, about Mike flying solo in a Vampire fighter and pulling 'g' in a tight turn—and the seat adjustment collapsed. Back in straight and level flight he wound the seat up to the top of its travel, and it clattered back down to the bottom again. All he could see was a patch of sky right above the aeroplane. He described having to land the Vampire standing up in the cockpit. Even in the Chipmunk Flt. Lt. Brooke had an extra cushion under his parachute.

---

[1] Flt. Lt. Mike Brooke has published at least two books. His first, A Bucket of Sunshine, is about flying a Canberra bomber during the Cold War. His second, Follow me Through, is about instructing cadets (like me) on the Chipmunk.

The Squadron bus would drop us at Scone airfield, a big grass airfield with a concrete parking area in front of the hangar, and a control tower. My allocated instructor was Flt. Lt. Hamish Logan, one of the older instructors with a receding hairline. On presenting myself to him he filled in a form and, when I told him my date of birth, he gave a pitiful groan with the realisation of impending old age. I was his first pupil of the Nineteen Fifties, signifying that another decade had slipped by.

The weather was poor early that year, and many days were unsuitable for flying so to begin with we learned the external inspection routine. Before every flight, every aeroplane undergoes an external inspection (or walkaround) by the pilot. Sometimes jokingly referred to as "kick the tyres," we systematically walked around clockwise, checking for any visible damage, fluid leaks, loose items, missing items, pitot covers or locks still fitted, snow and ice contamination, or any other reason to reject the aeroplane.

We were also shown how to check the parachute and how to exit the aircraft in an emergency in flight. During the Easter break I spent a whole week at Scone and flew every day. We started with air experience, how it felt to be airborne, "You feeling OK? Not going to throw up?"

Then we were shown the local area, and how to spot the home field. "See that really big field, bang in the centre of this big semi-circle of the river Tay?" Scone was easy to spot, and I never felt I could get myself lost there as the terrain was so distinctive.

We moved on to effects of controls, trying each control in turn in straight and level flight. Stick sideways moved the ailerons that started a bank which would increase to reach a deadly downward spiral. Rudder started a yaw, which turned into a bank that would increase to reach a deadly downward spiral. Elevator pushed the nose down into a dive, or pulled it up into a climb, you stalled, then entered a deadly dive, or spin. The only UP control was the throttle. Push it forward to go up. We taxied around in zigzag fashion as we could not see obstructions or obstacles past the nose (it's a taildragger) just like our heroes in Spitfires and Hurricanes.

Straight and level flight was not as easy as it looked. You pick a landmark on the horizon and fly towards it at 3000 feet, keeping the nose "just below the landmark, just there." But the commentary from the rear cockpit continued, "You are diving, stay at 3000!"

"You are wandering left."

"Stay at 3000."

"You are wandering right, and climbing." And so on. Turning almost seemed easy after that. Lower a wingtip to bank the wing and it turns, level the wings to stop banking and it stops turning, end of story. Maintaining height at the same time was tricky though. Then we moved on to throttle control, climbing and descending. Full power and raise the nose a little to climb, close the throttle and lower the nose to descend.

Every time we changed anything we had to re-trim, we adjusted the elevator trim control such that the aeroplane would fly 'hands off,' with no force on the control stick. The instructor would tell us to hold our hands right up where he could see them from behind, to prove that we really had trimmed it properly. Oh yes and, "Keep the ball in the middle!" all the time. We had to use the rudder to keep the ball centred in the curved tube of the slip indicator.

Three or four hours of that gave us the basic idea, but the weather turned. A couple of weekends were spent looking out at the rain in Scone. Someone with binoculars spotted a bird out on the airfield. Flt. Lt. Logan asked, "Is it walking or swimming?"

"It's a duck," a short pause, "and it's swimming," came the despondent reply, so flying was off again that day. It was about that time that I passed my driving test, thanks to parental generosity, but I didn't have a car.

The highlight of the Squadron year was summer camp, by which time I had a new instructor, Flt. Lt. Ian Montgomerie, as Hamish Logan had been posted elsewhere. For two weeks of our summer vacation we were sent to an RAF base somewhere else in the UK for more intensive flying training. Our commanding officer was a Wing Commander (unusual for a university squadron) who had enough clout to get Transport Command to fly us south in a Hastings, a transport aircraft with a tailwheel and four piston engines.

Our final destination was RAF Bicester in Oxfordshire, a grass airfield of the old style, like Scone, with a control tower and some old Beverley transports quietly rotting in the corner. We were to be housed, not in tents or barracks but two-in-a-room in the proper Officers' Mess where all our meals were provided. And we were allocated a "batman" who would wake us every morning with a cup of tea and a cheery word, and offer to polish our shoes. The idea of an allocated servant was strange to a working-class cadet, but I am sure the Eton/Oxbridge chaps would take to it quite naturally.

At summer camp the weather was good, the grass was dry and firm and we had plenty of flying. The Oxfordshire terrain seemed flat and featureless after Perthshire, and I found Bicester airfield hard to pick out from a distance, but fortunately we seldom strayed far. Every weekday we were training hard in the Chipmunk, mostly flying circuits, and more circuits. We would check the outside on the walkaround, check the cockpit, start the engine, and taxi to the take-off position.

Holding the stick back, we would smoothly push open the throttle to full power and, when a bit of speed registered on the ASI, push the stick forward just enough to raise the tail. Holding a level attitude by careful adjustment of the stick, we accelerated to take-off speed, on reaching which a slight ease back on the stick allowed the Chipmunk to fly itself off the runway, the bumping stops, and we are airborne. We climb at the correct speed, turn ninety degrees for a short time, then another turn takes us "downwind" on a level flightpath parallel to the runway.

We have more checks to perform in preparation for landing, then, judging the position carefully, a throttle reduction, two stages of flap and two further turns position us onto the approach path to the runway. Small throttle adjustments are needed so that touchdown would occur not too near the hedge and not too far into the field. When really low (you can see individual blades of grass) look ahead, close the throttle and progressively ease back on the stick and the Chipmunk settles on the grass in a nose high attitude, main wheels and tailwheel almost together. Then we could either taxi back for another take-off or keep the speed up to do a roller.

That means put the flap to the take-off position and open the throttle to take-off in the remaining runway. And round we would go for another circuit, and yet another until I consistently got it near enough right. At any moment the instructor could pull the throttle to idle and call "Fanstop" to simulate an engine failure. Don't panic, nose down, don't panic, pick a field, don't panic, speed-right, flap-down prepare for landing, then the throttle would open again and we would fly back into the circuit with a, "Not bad!" or "You nearly killed us there!"

On one circuit I was concentrating hard on lining up with the runway for landing but the instructor grabbed the stick to take control and said harshly, "Let the speed bleed off like that again on the final turn and you're DEAD!" A lesson never forgotten.

We flew every day except the weekend when awaydays in the squadron minibus to visit a Lightning or Hunter base were arranged, or we could buy a ride in a two-seat glider based on the field. The glider flights were an eerie experience. We were towed up to 2000 feet (by a local Chipmunk I think) and released. It was quiet, too quiet, reminding me of a permanent 'fanstop' emergency. I liked the reassurance of a propeller turning in front of me and the rumble of an old Gypsy Major. There is no "Up!" control in a glider.

In the second week of summer camp there occurred the single most momentous and significant event of my life to that point, and seldom surpassed until I became a dad. Flt. Lt. Montgomerie stopped the Chipmunk near the end of the runway and asked, "Could you do that again, just once, by yourself?"

"Yes Sir!" Then he climbed out of the rear cockpit, closed the canopy and walked off. THIS WAS IT. I checked that the canopy was locked, was cleared for take-off and one circuit by Tower. I expect they guessed my predicament from my faltering voice. I took off, flew a normal circuit round and landed, then taxied in and parked.

That went OK! It's not all that obvious there is nobody in the back, and I felt neither fear nor elation at the time. But that leap, from this riverbank where ordinary working people lived, took me onto the first stepping stone that would eventually lead to the faraway bank where airline pilots lived.

One or two other cadets soloed that day and, in the best RAF tradition, the evening of the first solo involved a visit to the bar in the Officers' Mess and a serious amount of drinking and silly games. In the interests of preserving tradition, when approaching my volumetric limit I switched to spirits and of course towards the end of the evening I threw up—another first for me as I had never drunk enough before to get drunk.

A couple of days later I was sent solo again by my instructor, who briefed me to go out to his aeroplane, perform the external check, call ATC for clearance, and fly 4 (I think) circuits, then taxi back, "And don't bend it!"

After starting the engine I found that the radio didn't work. Call after call for taxi clearance went unanswered, until I realised that the tower and their transmitter were directly on my left, and the receiver aerial was under the right wing, shielded by the rest of the aircraft. It then dawned on me that the green flashing light in the tower was for me, allowing me to taxi, and operated by someone a bit quicker-witted than I was. As soon as I turned out of the parking line I was back in radio contact.

Air Squadron flying was not all circuits. On a couple of flights towards the end of summer camp I was told to make my straps as tight as possible and was then taught some simple aerobatics, loops and rolls. We started by flying a circle to make sure we had a clear area and then settled flying along a straight line, a road or railway. I put the nose down in a gentle full-power dive, the speed increased to the entry speed of 130 knots and then I pulled, between 3 and 4 'g.' It feels quite dramatic at first. The nose of the Chipmunk soars to the sky and the blood rushes to your boots.

Airspeed decreases so that by the time you see the horizon again, upside down, speed is down to 70, 60, 50 as you float over the top pulling only just enough to keep the nose going round. After rounding the top the ground fills the view and you start pulling again to avoid it. You level out and hear a voice from behind, "Where has that straight railway line gone? Let's try that again, and check the wings level when you see the horizon at the top!"

Not long after that, soon after starting the second year of my degree, the news percolated through that the government's drastic cuts in the military budget would affect us. The squadron was to be cut to less than half its former strength, so only those who had already signed up for a career in the RAF were retained. I had already made it clear that the RAF was not for me.

The lifestyle involved getting posted every three years, often to an unpopular base or aircraft type, or even a desk job. Many RAF officers were married, and while some lived off the base in their own place, others lived in the RAF's "married quarters" which were temporary furnished accommodation in which the family didn't own as much as the teaspoons. Not ideal, I thought, for a family life rooted in the community.

Life without Aeroplanes

Life went on without aeroplanes. Second year Engineering was pretty challenging academically, as entry to the Aeronautics course depended upon passing all six exams first time, but with some serious study that worked out. Straight after the exams I started a job, packing biscuits on night shift in a biscuit factory where the basic rate wasn't great but we did long hours and had a night-shift bonus. It's amazing how quickly one tires of eating free biscuits, but that's a good thing. The aim was to buy a car, and a second-hand car dealer, a friend of a friend of my dad, picked out a "really good one" that turned out to be an Austin

A40 Farina. Hey, I had one of those years ago—a slot-car model one. The car was going to be very useful to get to this biscuit job, and also to pick up girls.

I had met Suzanne, the daughter of my aunt's friend, a few times over the previous ten years, but shortly before this job we had met again and she had shape-shifted, completely transformed into this gorgeous creature with long blond hair, a great bust, a tall slim figure and legs, from there all the way to the ground. She lived over an hour away using two buses with a good walk in between, but only seven miles, fifteen minutes in one's own car.

That made it viable, so I asked her out. She accepted! WOW! So started my education in cinema dates, romantic dinners, parking in quiet places and, yes, snogging. After several months she dumped me, but I was not too downhearted. After all, the ball was in play, I had reached first base, and was determined to continue to play the game. A few other girls were dated before I met "the one," my soulmate with whom I felt really compatible.

The Aero course at Glasgow was a bit dry, a bit theoretical, with plenty of theory and equations, but nothing much in the way of aeroplane shaped metal. It was a great relief then to be sent as part of our degree to the College of Aeronautics at Cranfield in Bedfordshire for a two-week course in Flight Testing. Andy, Brian, Robert and myself were the four from Glasgow on this course. I drove down in my new car, in case it proved useful.

We had lectures about aeroplane design and performance, then we had flights in a twin engined DH Dove during which we measured various flight parameters, then we returned to the classroom to calculate things about the Dove that we never knew before. It was really great to connect with aeroplanes again and remember why aeronautics was invented. The theory is just a means to an end, to get people flying machines, with a purpose in mind.

There was also the social aspect to consider at Cranfield. We met students from other British universities (all men) but there were women in the social club and Robert and I chatted up a couple who lived locally, and by the end of the evening we had arranged to pick them up and drive them to a pub on the Sunday (told you the car would be useful). That went well so an evening date was arranged for later in the week.

On date night we had some drinks in the bar (as driver I was on orange juice) and then someone suggested we go for a drive, and we ended up at a nice quiet spot and parked. Robert sat in the back with one girl, while Mary and I in the front seats started with a little gentle kissing, then progressed to some heavy snogging but after an hour or so we readjusted bras, buttons and zips and took them home.

I had made a friend in the year above my Aeronautics course, and he helped me get a summer job as a brickie's mate, moving bricks and mortar for the tradesmen repairing furnace linings. One job in particular had us working inside the furnace of a tube mill. The steel works shut down for 2 weeks in the summer when all the workers had their fixed "Glasgow Fair" holiday, and while we did repair and maintenance work in the furnaces.

They let them cool for a couple of days, helped by big cooling fans, but it was heavy work and we worked twelve-hour shifts, day and night. The tube furnace had a three-foot ceiling and our sweat boiled and hissed when it hit the floor that first day. The hard-earned money was enough to run the car for another year, and then some.

In my fourth and final year I eventually took more interest in sport, when I found a sport in which we participated lying down. That is a sport with my name all over it, and was called small-bore rifle shooting. On any given Monday evening maybe a dozen of us, men and women, gathered in the loft above a commercial garage, fired hundreds of 0.22 inch bore rim-fire long-rifle rounds at paper targets, then went to the nearby pub.

After a few weeks I saw my name on the Union notice-board listed as part of the team for a Saturday competition and thought, "Someone's having a laugh!" I refused to be tricked, but next club-night they wondered why I hadn't turned up. They were desperate as, apart from a few long-term medical students, most of the members had only just joined.

So from then on I spent one or two Saturdays a month travelling around Scotland to away matches against other universities, and generally we lost. It was good social interaction though, and sometimes I drove in my car with three other members, but no guns or ammunition as they were carried by committee members. On one trip I desperately needed to buy petrol, but we were running late so I agreed to put it off until right after the competition. But instead we had to follow someone else's car to find the nearby hotel for dinner, so it was to be right after dinner, then after the party, but when at last we set out all the garages had closed.

I drove on in desperation now, and we found a garage eventually where the owner lived on the premises and very kindly helped us out (and earned a big tip). Another time, late at night, a warning light came on along a quiet lonely road and the chap sitting in front with me checked under the bonnet. "Fan belt's broken, could you girls in the back slip off your tights?" Shocked, suspicious silence. "That's the standard emergency substitute! Honest."

But both girls wore jeans for shooting, without tights. The engine ran hot, though acceptably so, and I thought we would make it. I dropped the others in the city and headed home, but after a while the lights started to dim as the battery ran down. I resorted to using moonlight with just the occasional flash of lights at bends and junctions from there to my home, and just made it with the engine misfiring badly by then.

My big chance came at the BUSF (British Universities Sports Federation) competition in Wembley when I shot for Glasgow, and we came 13th out of 26 Universities, and last among the Scottish ones taking part. The senior members of the club were despondent, but hey! I was there.

For an Honours degree we had to write a final year Thesis, a daunting prospect early on, but I got through it under the supervision of Dr A.W. Babister. I experimented on and wrote about yaw-heads (What's that? Who cares?). I earned my second-class Hon. B.Sc. and that's what counted for graduation. My parents proudly attended the ceremony.

Chapter 2
College of Air Training, Hamble

Applications for the College of Air Training at Hamble were sent there directly and the interviews and selection procedures all took place there, apart from one of the medicals. Getting a place in the College, sponsored and paid for by BEA/BOAC was not easy. The selection process for entry to the College was long and multi-faceted. First there was the application form, completed in the knowledge that for every thousand forms sent in, something like four applicants graduated as pilots.

However I was summoned to interview during which I was asked about my background and education. I could imagine them ticking off the boxes; a long-term interest in aviation, the family connection, the aeronautics degree and of course primarily the solo time in the University Air Squadron. I made sure I told them about representing my University in a national sporting competition as well. I was asked why I wanted to be a pilot and why BEA/BOAC.

Then we were all seated in an exam room and asked to fill in forms containing hundreds of simple looking multi-choice questions (written and marked by psychologists) which had to be completed very quickly, so answers had to be based on first impressions. Then we progressed to aptitude tests. There were tests of co-ordination, general physical and mental ability, and a strange one in which we took one pencil in each hand and moved them alternately, left hand then right, from one small circle to the next on a long roll of paper, in time with a series of seemingly random clicks from a tape recorder. Sometimes it was impossible to keep up. I learned later that just doing one's best was fine, but smashing the pencils or throwing them at a member of staff in a fit of rage would be a fail.

The next stage of the application process was a standard pilot medical, followed by a more thorough medical, more stringent than for qualified pilots, as the airline was paying our way and didn't want to waste their investment on people whose fitness standards were already borderline and might deteriorate. Cadets with glasses were virtually unheard of.

The final stage of selection included a group task, for which applicants were divided into groups of five or six and seated around a round table. The task given to the group to which I was allocated was to organise a rally team whose objective was to overcome supply and logistics difficulties to get a rally car from A to B. We had to use fuel consumption figures to calculate fuel required, work out where and how to get the needed supplies and transport them to where they would be used.

Several small simple calculations were needed so I took it upon myself to start the ball rolling by allocating tasks among the group. After a few minutes the results were collected and a plan began to emerge, was discussed and agreed upon. Our solution to the problem was handed in to the interview panel, and immediately shot down as we had planned to siphon fuel from a diesel van to use in a rally car.

That did not seem to matter as I was later told I had passed and would be considered for a course sometime in the future. I think that I passed because I showed leadership potential in trying to organise the group and break the problem into small individual tasks. I was maybe lucky that I was the oldest of the group, the only graduate, and had a rough idea of what they wanted. That was another successful leap, and another steppingstone closer to my goal.

I do not think I would have been accepted straight from school at seventeen. I think my acceptance was based on the group task performance, and the fact I had flown and been sent solo in the University Air Squadron, plus of course my added maturity having successfully completed a four-year course at University.

I also applied for several jobs in engineering during final year, and attended several interviews with British aircraft manufacturers, BEA Engineering and the Civil Service. However in 1971 the British aircraft industry was in dire straits, with few civil or military aircraft being designed, thus not many jobs were available.

After several rejections I was eventually offered one of those jobs, provisional on gaining a second-class honours degree, and I had accepted it when the exam results came out. A few days later the letter arrived from Hamble inviting me to join a course in January 1972 and I accepted immediately. I then wrote to my potential employer to say, with humble apologies, that I had changed my mind about their job offer.

The College of Air Training at Hamble was owned by, and organised on behalf of, the two state owned airlines, BEA and BOAC, so everything was done to suit them. The Principle, and nearly all the flying instructors and lecturers, were ex-RAF and they knew their stuff, but as a result the College felt like a cross between a public school and RAF Cranwell (though I had experience of neither).

Hamble was a large grass airfield near Southampton on a little peninsula sticking down into the Solent. It had a large number of student accommodation blocks in which the students were housed in single rooms, with five or six sharing the toilets, washroom and showers in each hallway. I'd say it had been designed with all-male occupancy in mind. (The modern co-ed Colleges have en-suite accommodation).

There were of course the usual aviation premises; hangars where the aircraft were kept and serviced, offices, briefing rooms where we met our instructors each flying day and they explained the day's lesson, before and after the flight, and there were classrooms in which we had lectures about all sorts of aviation related topics. We were taught some aerodynamics, to a level far above that in the Air Squadron, but way below that in my Aeronautics degree.

We learned aviation law, aviation meteorology, radio for communications and navigation, aircraft instruments, navigation (general, planning and plotting), signals (including Morse code), propulsion (props and jets), aircraft systems, aircraft load and balance, aircraft performance and so on.

Hamble also had a torture chamber which contained a number of boxes in which students could be locked for an hour or two at a time, sweating profusely even in winter. We were supposed to be in these Link Trainers to learn procedural flying on instruments, but their real purpose was to gratify the sadists who operated them and made us suffer. The Link Trainer was like an aircraft cockpit covered by an opaque canopy, fitted with controls which made the whole device flop from side to side, rotate round and round and pitch up and down, on its pneumatically motivated mounting. Meanwhile the instruments inside told the student in the vaguest of terms where the airfield and its radio beacons might be.

We also had classes called "liberal studies," a sort of social awareness program, and that had been added so that Hamble qualified as an educational rather than a training establishment. That gave them some tax breaks apparently. It also meant that students could claim some subsistence and travel expenses like any other student, means tested against parents' income. Ah yes, those were the good old days of free education and student grants: the post-war baby boomer generation had it easy.

Out in the hangar the College kept a large collection of aircraft, mainly Piper Cherokee trainers with four seats and a 180 HP engine. The student pilot sat in the left seat with the instructor on his right, with dual controls. The disadvantage of this was that the student could not see out to the right very well, a problem when solo. Sometimes an instructor would take a second student in the rear seats when flying to another airfield for training variety. The Cherokee was said to be easy to fly, 'designed to suit the wives of American farmers' was the phrase I heard.

Instead of the traditional 'fighter' control column, it had a control yoke, like a small steering wheel (with the top cut away) for roll control, mounted on a tube that slid in and out of the lower instrument panel for elevator control. The student used it left-handed, in conjunction with the throttle in the centre of the panel. The fleet also included a few DHC Chipmunks which were needed to teach spins and spin recovery as the Cherokee was not cleared for spinning. For the later part of the course, twin engine rating, night flying and airways flying, they had Beechcraft Barons which had six seats, powerful six-cylinder engines and retractable undercarriage. They were considered to be a very classy and high performance (and expensive) training twin.

My course at Hamble was numbered 721, being the first course of 1972, and for administrative convenience was split into three sections, A, B and C. Each section's classroom for groundschool held sixteen students, seemingly selected at random from the total course of forty-eight. Two courses had been cancelled in the latter part of 1971, and no more started until autumn in 1972, so we considered ourselves privileged to be selected for a course at all. About half of course 721 were university graduates, most had some flying experience, and several had experience of flying model aeroplanes, like me.

Getting through the course was not easy. For the first fourteen weeks we did nothing but groundschool, culminating in exams in all subjects. We were never near an aeroplane. I found groundschool no problem, as I already had a degree in passing exams, but one of our number who had plenty of flying experience could not cope with exams and had to leave the course. Pilots just have to pass exams. I did not take to the flying as easily. Rumour had it that the Cherokee was easy to land compared to the old taildragger Chipmunks, with their peculiar handbrake system.

With a Cherokee you were supposed to be able to plonk it down on the mainwheels, lower the nosewheel and apply the brakes to slow down, and the nosewheel was guaranteed to keep the prop off the runway, give steering control, and let you see out of the front window. But in addition to struggling to fly precise heights, headings and tracks, I now found I had trouble landing as well. I was never much good with my left hand.

One cadet was sent home from my Hamble course as he didn't go solo. Two down, forty-six left. We had seen the warning signs. After quite a number of hours' instruction without being sent solo, he had a flight with the chief flying instructor, then he was given a different instructor and several more hours of instruction, so when he again flew with the CFI without going solo it was no surprise to hear that he was packing to go home. We knew that any of us could 'get the chop,' any time.

I got the hang of landing Cherokees in the end though. I was sent up for my first solo in under 12 hours, which was acceptable, and that night I got drunk again in the best RAF tradition (and threw up again). I decided it was a pointless tradition and never did it again. Local flying consisted of taking off from Hamble and flying circuit after circuit, or heading over to the Isle of Wight to practise all the other exercises like medium turns, steep turns, stalling, unusual attitudes, forced landing and so on.

Engine failure, we had learned in aerodynamics class, does not mean that you fall out of the sky since all aeroplanes can glide, even the heaviest. The engine does not lift, it pushes, and pushing the wing forward gives lift. At any time the instructor could close the throttle for a practice forced landing. Then we lower the nose to point downhill, so that, like a car on a slope, the aircraft's weight contributes forward thrust and it becomes a glider. The drill is to start a glide at optimum gliding speed, then pick a field nearby, somewhere level and unobstructed, pointing into wind for preference.

Then comes the Big Question, "Are we going to make it?" The answer is plain to see. If your aiming point is moving up the windscreen, you will not make it. If it is moving down the windscreen you will overfly it. The piece of ground that seems to hold steady on a mark on the windscreen is where you will arrive. With practice we learn to tell at a glance whether or not we will make the field.

(Incidentally, that's how Captain Sullenberger would know instantly that he could not make a runway and had to ditch in the Hudson).

We had a go at flying "under the hood," which was a device worn on the student's head which restricted his view to the instrument panel and inside the cockpit. We had to learn to fly solely by interpreting the instruments. To check our progress the instructor would cover the student's face as well, manoeuvre the aircraft into an "unusual attitude," then uncover his face and say, "Recover!" We then had to read the instruments to see what was happening to the aircraft and work out which way it was pointing, and then apply control inputs to get back to straight and level flight.

Their most cunning ploy was to apply left bank very gradually while your face was covered, maybe pitch the nose down a little, then roll right abruptly to level the wings and say, "Recover!" All our senses screamed that we were in a right bank, a spiral dive with the speed increasing, but the instruments showed wings level. You really have to steel yourself to believe the instruments, ease the nose up, and ignore the banking right sensations. Believing the instruments, not your senses, is a very important lesson.

The Isle of Wight, unlike Bicester in Oxfordshire, was a great local flying area as it was impossible to get lost. Having a coastline all around and a pointy north end at Cowes made it easy to know where we were at all times, find our way to the departure point, then fly towards the Fawley chimney on the mainland and over to the Hamble peninsula which stood out very well, even in marginal weather.

My first room at Hamble was ground floor, but as senior courses graduated other rooms became available and I moved upstairs to a room overlooking the swimming pool, which was unheated and so used in the summer only. In springtime I watched it being cleaned out and filled with clear clean new water that looked so inviting. I put on my swimming trunks, wandered down and jumped in.

The cold had me all but paralysed, but with a huge effort I managed to surface and swim a length, struggle out at the shallow end and jog back to my block for a hot shower. The pool did warm up acceptably later in the summer, but the most frequent user was George Florence who was on a later course than mine and was a champion canoeist, frequently to be seen in his kayak in the pool endlessly practising rolling inverted, and back upright again, and manoeuvring between and around a couple of sticks he had set up suspended from a wire above the pool. I was impressed when I saw on the news that his son David won silver (again) for the UK in the 2012 London Olympic Games, in the canoe slalom event (and again recently in Rio).

My flying instructor Captain Gilbert once told me that it is never a good idea to argue in flight. It was acceptable to discuss options, but any heated argument should be saved for the ground, once the flight was safely completed. While the aircraft commander can always over-rule the copilot, when the captain is flying it is the copilot's duty to tell him if he believes that they are in danger. In those circumstances the copilot needs to be assertive and the captain must take heed and change his intended flight path to a safer option, without starting an argument. Several accidents have proved that it is too easy to forget the cardinal rule. Someone must concentrate on flying the aeroplane safely at all times.

At university we had been used to getting the summer off, from early June until early October, so it came as something of a shock, even to the school leavers, to confront our summer break, a fixed three-week shutdown of the College in August.

I packed my bags on the Saturday morning and took the train to London, where I met up with my girlfriend Anne who had just arrived from Glasgow. We then jetted off from Gatwick on a package tour to a lovely new hotel in a quiet little resort in Mallorca for a fun-filled ten-day holiday. The resort had a quiet little beach, a bar and a few shops, plus a bus service to Palma and the bigger resorts and tourist attractions around the island. As a side note, I proposed to Anne the following year after getting my pilot's licence and we returned to that same hotel for a short holiday, forty-two years later, on her birthday. The resort was much busier, but it was a nice nostalgia trip.

After the summer break we moved on to navigation, getting from A to B, and that involved looking at the map, planning a route using easily identified landmarks, measuring the tracks and distances between waypoints and estimating the headings and timings needed, knowing the airspeed and forecast wind that day. The Isle of Wight was too easy, so for the first exercise we set off north-east from Hamble for a small town called Wickham, our first landmark or waypoint. The next waypoint we called Meon Crossroads, about nine nautical miles to the NNE. As we set off from Wickham at two or three thousand feet Captain Gilbert said, "Do you see this valley that we are following? That's called the Meon Valley."

And I replied, "No, I don't see a valley. Valleys are Vee shaped, with sloping sides, and this is all flat."

"Well do you see the river we are following, with the road alongside?"

"Oh yes, no problem."

"Well humour me, let's just call this road out of Wickham the Meon Valley, and that right angled cross-roads up ahead, with the building at it, is Meon Crossroads. OK? That is our next waypoint where our cross-country trips begin and end."

"Yes, fine by me!—Sir," I replied not wanting to sound argumentative or cheeky.

Over the next few weeks I set off on visual navigation exercises, always starting with Hamble-Wickham-Meon Crossroads, and always ending with the same familiar arrival procedure. I can honestly say that I was never lost, and each time the stopwatch said we should be over Meon Crossroads I could look around and down, and there it was. Sometimes I was flying with Captain Gilbert, sometimes I was solo and occasionally we had a 'mutual' navigation exercise with another student.

On one of these I set off with Mick, a close friend and neighbour, as he lived across the corridor in the same accommodation block. We set off for Birmingham Airport in weather that was good at Hamble and forecast to be adequate at destination. When we arrived the weather was indeed adequate, just. We reported to 'Big C,' the office by the control tower bearing on the outside a large black letter C on a yellow background, where we announced our arrival and filled in departure paperwork. Looking upwind, the weather looked a bit ominous with bad visibility and rainstorms on radar moving in, so we decided to depart immediately, rushed back to the Cherokee, called ATC and hastily departed. We just managed to creep out of Birmingham, checking visual references and trying to reassure each other that we were indeed just about legally visual with the ground and potential traffic. We were talking to Approach and in radar cover of course so it was all perfectly safe, and we made it back to Hamble no bother.

We also practised navigation exercises "under the hood" so that all flying and navigating was on instruments, and to confirm your position you had quickly to take bearings from two radio beacons. Where the lines crossed was your position. An instructor or another student had to be there to watch all around for other traffic. We also practised diversions, wherein during a carefully planned navigation exercise the instructor would say, "I've changed my mind, let's go to Thruxton instead!" Then I would have to plot our position on my map, draw a line from there to Thruxton (in this example) measure the track and allow for wind-drift then set off. He also wanted an estimated arrival time, the pedant.

During this first summer a tragic event took place that was to have a profound effect on our future training. A BEA Trident crashed near Staines when climbing out of Heathrow. The story that emerged later was that the two junior co-pilots were scared to contradict or question a very irritable senior captain, and while he was having a suspected heart attack somebody moved the droop lever up instead of the flap lever and the resulting deep stall killed everyone.

Another incident that made an impression on all of the cadets at Hamble was the time when one of my course-mates was flying solo in a Cherokee and the engine stopped. We often practised engine failure followed by a pretend forced landing and we were all familiar with the drill. Convert excess airspeed to height, glide at the recommended speed, pick a field free from obstructions and plan a descent towards the field for a rough-field landing.

Of course in our practice sessions we always opened the throttle at a safe height and climbed away. But young Nick was not so lucky and finished up landing in his chosen field at a rate of knots, with insufficient room to stop before hitting the fence. That stopped his Cherokee abruptly. The damaged aeroplane was brought back to the hangar where we could all see it, and learn. Fortunately Nick was deemed to have done his best, and so he continued on the course.

During the single engined flying, three hours were spent in a Chipmunk, to let us try a taildragger and see what it was like to taxi and fly, but mainly to fulfil the legal requirements for spinning and recovery. There was no time for fun aerobatics. In the second year of the course the flying began to tail off and we had more groundschool, culminating in the final exams, following which we moved on to big boys' toys, the powerful twin engined Beechcraft Barons.

The controls in the Baron were like the Cherokee, with the addition of prop levers for the variable pitch props. They had retractable undercarriage and some other refinements for radio navigation on Airways, and were based at Hurn airport, Bournemouth, as the grass field at Hamble was hard on retracting undercarriage. Hurn was also better equipped for night and bad weather flying. Initially we flew visually, to get the hang of the aeroplane with its greater complexity and power, and we practised engine failure, followed by single engined flying instead of a forced landing.

I was sent up solo for some general handling practice, including shutting down and restarting an engine. I was in that cocky stage, I'm sure we all get there, when I thought, "I can do this, I've really got this sussed, let's see just how quick I can be." I sat there and thought, "OK, practice engine failure of the…left engine. Go." I went through the well-practised memorised drill. I don't remember it now exactly but it went something like Throttle lever, prop lever, mixture lever, ignition switches, fuel tap. And both engines stopped! Yikes!

It went really quiet, with just the whooshing of the airflow outside, and my pounding heartbeat. After a couple of seconds, I went back through the same actions but in reverse, and both engines restarted. YES! Result! Hardly descended at all. I think I then practised it, with care, a couple of times, but keep all this to yourself as I never told anyone, until now. But often in the years that followed when a British Airways trainer in the simulator said, "Take your time, sit on your hands, and make sure you identify the problem correctly first time: you don't want to shut down the wrong engine," I silently agreed wholeheartedly. Especially when that Midland B737 crashed on the motorway near Kegworth just short of East Midlands airport in 1989.

Another time I was solo in a Baron, flying to some other airfield for some general circuit practice, and I had the books open on the right seat to check radio frequencies and runway details of my destination airfield. The let-down book was loose leafed with the binding at the top so that individual pages could be renewed to update the book. I was doing some general handling as well and looking out for other traffic. While just rearranging the books on the unoccupied right seat I heard a loud "rat-tat-tat tat tat tat-tat" sound. A machine gun, on my tail!? Impossible, but I looked back anyway. What the hell then?

I placed a hand on the let-down book while looking behind again and the sound stopped, and I discovered the cause of the alarming noise. The book had been moved allowing a sheet of paper to creep outside through the gap between the door and its frame, and it had been flapping madly in the airflow, and flapped itself to bits.

The course continued with more emphasis on airways and instrument flying, procedural flying using multiple radio beacons, flying abroad (yes, to France), plus visual night circuits at Hamble without radio aids, and visual night navigation, dual and solo, going by the map and the pattern of city lights and destination airport lights. The huge hurdle at the end of our twin flying course was our Instrument Rating flight test which involved (if I remember correctly) flying from A to B on instruments, then entering the hold at B, followed by a let-down and overshoot, then doing the last bit again on one engine.

An outside examiner, from the CAA, was sent in for these final tests. One of my course-mates failed this final test twice, and was sent packing, but I managed to scrape through first time. After passing all of that we graduated from College with a 'frozen' ATPL. The Commercial pilot's licence had different levels, and we had passed all the exams for the top level (needed to be a Captain) and just needed to accumulate the hours and experience which would automatically entitle us to convert from the basic licence to the top level ATPL. I had taken another successful leap. The rosy glow of that riverbank lined with airline pilots was close now.

Chapter 3
Aviation in General CAA Rules

This book is not intended for airline pilots, who would find it boring, maybe even pretentious. So for the general public with a bit of interest in aviation here is some general information about how civil aviation works. Check out the Glossary at the end too. Civil aviation is ruled by a branch of government known in the UK as the CAA or Civil Aviation Authority (like the FAA in the USA). They issue the pilot licences, they regulate aircraft design, they regulate airlines, they regulate airports and Air Traffic Control (ATC), they even regulate model aeroplanes to an extent (of their choice).

Runways use a numbering system based on their direction. The direction along the centreline, in degrees using a magnetic compass, is rounded to the nearest 10 degrees. Drop the last zero to leave two digits and that's the runway number, which is painted on the end of the runway. Sometimes there is a Right or Left after it, as at Heathrow which has the two parallel runways 27L and 27R when taking off directly west.

If the wind is easterly we take off the other way, to the east, and the same runways are renumbered as 09R and 09L. We try to take-off and land into wind, so if the wind is coming from the west, left to right on the weather map, we take off to the west, right to left, on runway 27.

Airliners plan to fly along Airways, which are like highways in the sky and normally go from one radio beacon to the next. They are used for planning, but ATC in most of the UK, Europe and North America uses radar, and the radar controller would often give route changes, or "go direct XYZ" where XYZ was a radio beacon further along the planned route. In some busy areas in the USA they dispensed with the airways and the controller instructs the pilot to fly headings and altitudes.

Short haul flying involved taking off, following the prescribed departure procedure or SID (standard instrument departure), then under autopilot control on to the next radio beacon, then the next and so on until arriving close to the destination where we followed a standard arrival (or STAR). Often the STAR would include a holding pattern. This was a radio beacon where, at busy times when there were too many arrivals at once for ATC to cope with, arriving aircraft would be told to hold at the beacon (or enter the 'stack'). That involved flying a prescribed oval or "race-track" pattern with a specific track towards the beacon and left or right turn as specified. There could be many aircraft in the stack, or holding pattern, each 1000 feet above the other though it looks closer, especially when turning. As the bottom aircraft was cleared for its approach and taken out under radar control, each aircraft in the hold would be moved down one level.

The approach usually consists of radar control to the ILS or Instrument Landing System, a three-dimensional approach path. At busy airports there is a complex radio beam transmitted exactly along the centreline of the runway and out for twenty odd miles, together with a beam exactly 3 degrees up from the horizontal. Cockpit instruments tell us whether to go left, right, up or down to get exactly on this approach path. And the autopilot can be programmed to follow the beams very precisely.

The best quality radio beams were Category 3 (Cat 3) and could be used for automatic landing in thick fog with a decision height of just 12 feet, or even zero. Less sophisticated ILS equipment, both in the aeroplane and on the airport, were called Category 1 (Cat 1) and we could not descend below 200 feet, our decision height, unless we could see the runway and its lights well enough to land manually from there (about half a mile out).

Some airports don't have even the basic Cat 1 ILS and that's where pilots have to earn their money the old-fashioned way. If we can see the runway or its lights from miles away and a good safe height then we can hand fly a visual approach as we did on training aircraft. But in rain, snow, low cloud and poor visibility we have to fly on instruments, and usually by hand, on a VOR/DME or NDB approach. These radio beams are generally not suitable for autopilots to follow. They are also less accurate so the minimum safe descent height, the 'decide' point from which we must see the runway, is higher and farther away.

We call 'Decide' for a VOR/DME roughly 400 feet and over a mile from the runway, and if using an NDB (in the bad old days) 600 feet and almost two miles out (ballpark figures). Coming soon to a lonely airfield near you, we are told, are accurate autopilot approaches guided by SatNav. But sometimes we are told to expect things decades before it actually happens.

Each runway at an airport has its own guidance system, or ILS. Other radio aids include the NDB (non-directional beacon) which just transmits a simple signal that a direction-finder in the aircraft points to, or the VOR which transmits a coded signal which gives its position accurately to the aircraft, usually with a distance-away code from the DME (distance measuring equipment).

Radar is extensively used, both in national coverage, airport specific coverage (approach control) and, at a few selected airports, precision approach radar (PAR) for accurate approaches or talk-downs. PAR allows even the most basic aircraft to use detailed instructions from a suitably qualified controller to get visual with the runway through bad weather.

Longhaul flying was just the same, but on flights across oceans, deserts or the like there would be a long segment in the middle with no radio beacons so aircraft would navigate using inertial navigation systems, backed up with GPS (SatNav) and VOR/DME radio aids. Before these electronic devices were invented navigators had to use charts and plot their course backed up with sun or star sightings using a sextant, and cockpits had a little glass dome for taking sightings, but that's Hamble teaching and used before my time, so least said the better. Trans-Atlantic flights use a set of fixed tracks with waypoints at whole-number latitude and longitude intersections after the last radio aids had been passed, and before they were reached on the other side.

Airline pilots in the UK are subject to constant checking. In the simulator (normally) or in an empty aeroplane they are checked in all the emergency procedures not normally encountered, and that happens twice a year. Then each year a check pilot sits in on a normal trip to make sure everything is being done "by the book." Then there is the annual book exam in which each pilot answers a questionnaire to make sure that he knows the aircraft and company manuals well enough.

Add to that two thorough CAA medicals per year and the CAA exams they have to pass when changing to a new aeroplane, and you realise that pilots have to be able to pass exams as well as fly. Flying could be a chancy business, and though failing a check or exam always left room for a re-sit, failing a medical could be career-ending. When I joined it was customary to take out insurance against failing a medical and losing that all-important licence. In later years a pay deal in BA included a loss of medical compensation making the insurance unnecessary for us.

Seats and Controls

In an airliner the Captain sits on the left with his own controls and instruments, and the co-pilot sits on the right with identical controls and instruments. Each has a control wheel for left/right up/down control, and foot operated rudder pedals with wheel brake controls operated by pressing down with the toes. The rudders on a jet are used only to keep straight on the runway, to kick off drift just before touchdown, and in the event of an engine failure to counteract the asymmetric thrust. In normal flight they are just footrests and must not be moved. Aggressive and unnecessary rudder use led to an Airbus crash in New York in 2001.

There used to be an additional seat for third pilot/engineer (Trident, L1011, old 747). Extra seats (sometimes called jump-seats) are fitted, sometimes as cunningly hidden fold-down seats, for additional pilots (supervising, training, checking, heavy). The throttles, engine and standby instruments, airbrake lever, parking brake, flap and undercarriage controls are in the middle where both pilots can reach. Things like the radio tuning boxes and other controls are placed in the centre console between the pilots along with each pilot's FMC, flight management computer. And above the centre console there would be a roof panel containing controls for air conditioning, electrical and hydraulic systems, fuel pumps and fuel contents gauges, anti-icing systems and so on.

The two pilots' instruments use different sources so they can be cross-checked and there is usually a basic third set to settle any arguments as to whose is correct. The autopilot controls are usually on the edge of the cockpit coaming above the instruments, along with knobs and windows for setting required altitude, speed and heading. These are reminders when hand flying, or the autopilot will use them as programmed.

Most (maybe all) jet airliners are fitted with autothrottle, which is like cruise control in cars. The pilot can set a desired speed in a window and the autothrottle will control the engines to try to stick to the selected speed. It is not mandatory for autoland and cruise, but we would use it if possible. When hand flying an approach it was often easier to disengage autothrottle and control the throttles manually. The autopilot would fly to the speed set in the speed window with throttles set, manually or automatically, to climb power or idle.

Inertial Navigation systems are fitted to modern jets, usually in triplicate in the overhead panel. They are initially programmed with the start position, the parking gate. They were prone to wander however and by the end of a trans-Atlantic flight they could be 5 or 10 miles out, so they were updated automatically by radio aids and/or GPS (SatNav). They fit three of each and use the average, unless one is very inaccurate in which case the other two will vote it out of the system. The Inertial Nav units feed their data to Flight Control computers; each pilot has his own, either of which can be selected to control the autopilot. Much pre-flight time is spent programming the flight computers with the aircraft load, fuel and route details.

Airliners carry radar, but it cannot display other aircraft. It is weather radar, designed to reflect from concentrations of water droplets in clouds. The thicker the concentration of droplets, the bigger the cloud and worse the turbulence inside. So the weather radar scans the sky ahead from side to side and displays coloured patches where the worst of the weather might be. I say might, as it is not a perfect science, and does not show clear air turbulence, or CAT.

Weather radar can usually be adjusted to look downward to maybe pick up coastlines or other prominent land features. In the modern glass cockpits the return from the weather radar can be superimposed on the map, or position, display. When yellow or red blips and blobs appear, pilots do whatever they can to avoid flying through or even close to them. Of course in daytime if we can see the big, towering clouds, the cumulonimbus which are the worst for turbulence, we will fly between them visually like flying along canyons in the sky.

The standard language used in aviation is English, a lucky break for us Brits, but it has become American English. So although when I started flying, aeroplanes had retracting undercarriage which was selected up on an overshoot, now airplanes have landing gear (or just gear) which is raised in the event of a go-around. In British Airways at least, American aviation terms became the norm, as all the Boeing and Lockheed manuals were written in American English. In foreign places like France you will hear English and French spoken on the radio, in Germany just English and in America they don't understand English, just American. A flight number like 1079 in Europe is "one zero seven nine," but in American it's "ten seventy-nine."

The Tech Log book is part of the aeroplane, which may not fly without it. It is a condensed history of the aircraft and can tell an oncoming Captain all he needs to know about any recent or recurring faults, what corrective action has been taken and what precautionary action he might need to take. For example if a main engine-driven generator does not work he may still fly back to base if he keeps the APU running (an auxiliary small turbine fitted to provide air-conditioning and electrical power on the ground). The Tech Log also records the history of fuel, engine oil and hydraulics consumption. The cabin crew have their own book to record defective reading lights or coffee makers.

Flight Planning

The first task for the pilots before a flight is to check the weather, at departure, at and around the destination, and on the way, then normally a computer-generated flight plan is produced, which the pilots check for accuracy, especially the fuel calculation. Fuel usage depends upon weight, the heavier the aircraft the more it burns and that's why we don't just "fill her up." Adding unnecessary weight limits the aircraft's "ceiling," the height to which it can climb, and results in increased fuel consumption.

Working backwards, we start with the total weight of the aircraft without fuel, add enough fuel for 45 minutes low level circling time, then add the fuel it takes to get from destination to the alternate. That's an airport near enough the destination with guaranteed better than adequate weather,—somewhere you can bank on. Then add the fuel from departure to destination, then add taxi fuel. The Captain looks at all these figures and uses his experience and judgement to adjust as necessary (like for expected delays) and orders the fuel he wants. Sometimes the co-pilot is asked to handle the flight, and he gets to do all these things, which is how he acquires experience and judgement, but he can always be over-ruled by the Captain.

Once a flight departs, the pilot is committed to carrying on with it until he lands somewhere and applies the parking brake. But there are limits on how long he can PLAN to fly. The limits depend on a great many factors including the time of day or night, how many take-offs he has done already that day, and so on. The limits may be extended using extra pilots or "heavy crew." The heavy crew sit in the additional cockpit seats for take-off and landing, they help out by performing tasks like the pre-flight walkaround or checking the books and maps, and they can check weather reports and look up the manuals for performance data if the runway changes. The main purpose of the heavy crew is to take the seats of the crew who do the take-off and landing (the operating crew) while they rest in a seat or bunk in a quiet area, extending their permitted hours. As aircraft achieve greater and greater range this is becoming more common on long-haul flights.

Flight time limitations are not the same for all, however. Each country can set its own, and the UK limits were quite sensible, while the British Airways negotiated limits were even more sensible. Other countries had quite lax, sometimes frightening limits on the hours crew worked, and I heard of several ways in which certain airlines used to circumvent the regulations. I don't like to worry you, but you don't want to fly with over-tired pilots. Company managers working 9 to 5 in air-conditioned offices are constantly trying to persuade regulators to relax the regulations. If you ever hear of a pilot strike in support of flight time limitations remember it is your lives they are trying to protect, as well as their own.

Pilots do not get proper meal breaks. Meals are often served in the cockpit and eaten from a tray on our lap while still flying on autopilot. If time permits the Captain and co-pilot will take it in turn to eat, but on short flights like Heathrow to Paris all eat together in the few minutes of stable flight between the departure procedure and the briefing and descent. The cabin crew will bring in two or three different meals, or on longer flights a menu from which to make choices of what to eat and when. Sometimes we would defer the meal to the turnaround time on the ground between short flights, but it was still a rush.

Most airliner flying is done on the autopilot, for convenience. All pilots take off manually as that has not yet been automated, but the autopilot is permitted to be engaged within a minute of leaving the ground. We don't normally do that, except for practice or to show it can be done, as it is generally easier to fly by hand until the flaps are up and the normal climb mode is established, then the autopilot is engaged somewhere around 5000 to 10000 feet altitude.

On arrival some pilots disengage the autopilot when leaving the holding beacon (only a masochist hand flies a hold) and the aircraft is flown manually all the way to landing. It is good for practice. But at the end of a long tiring flight many pilots will not throw away the autopilot until the runway is clearly visible, the aircraft is set up for landing and the checks are complete—about two minutes before landing.

Jet engines, including propeller-turbine engines (propjets), are slow to accelerate from idle. They idle at the lowest rotation speed at which they are stable and at which they burn least fuel. But it can take five to ten seconds to accelerate from idle speed to full power, and most of this delay is at the bottom end. On take-off we never go from idle straight to full power, as one engine could get to full power several seconds before the other which would make life difficult.

It is normal to open the throttles initially to 25% power, watch them both stabilise together, and then go for full power. On short runways or in bad weather conditions we would do this while holding stationary with the toe-brakes, then release brakes as we open up to full power. From 25% to 100% power takes only a couple of seconds.

All airliners have what are called "high lift devices," flaps at the rear of the wing for 60 to 80% of its length, plus (usually) leading edge slats or droop right along the front of the wing. Nowadays these are combined on one control lever, the flap lever, the first notch of which pushes out and down the front of the wing (slats) and then the next two, three or four notches progressively move the flaps at the rear of the wing aft and down. The slats and first one or two stages of flap allow the aircraft to fly more slowly, which makes take-off and landing safer.

The final stage of flap when they are angled down more steeply is for extra drag on landing. We want extra drag on approach so that we can counteract it with power from the engines. Instead of being at idle the engines have to be up at 25% power to counter the drag, so that in the event of a go-around they zip quickly to full power, the flaps go to take-off position and the landing gear goes up. With much less drag and full power the aircraft climbs quickly and safely away.

A typical take-off sequence (Captain flying) would start with clearance from ATC including a wind check, the co-pilot's confirmation that checks are complete and the wind is within limits then, on lining up, the throttles are opened to about 25% power. When the engines stabilise at that, the co-pilot would call "stable," the throttles would go to take-off power, the co-pilot calls "power set" and then passing (usually) 80 knots he calls "80 knots" then "V1" at a predetermined speed. That's the speed when you are committed. After that there is not enough runway left to stop.

At the next predetermined speed the co-pilot calls "Rotate," and the Captain pulls back on the controls to pull the nose up. Usually runways are long enough to stop from any speed up to Rotate so the call becomes a composite "V1-Rotate." When safely climbing the co-pilot calls "positive climb" to which the Captain responds, "gear up." At any time before the V1 call either pilot will call "STOP" (yes, that loudly) if he spots a significant problem, like a speed discrepancy at 80 knots, an engine over-temperature or under-power, or a fire. Once stopped, they will briefly discuss and agree what the problem was and how to deal with it.

The wind, and its effect on aeroplanes, has been a hotly debated subject and there are many misconceptions (even amongst pilots). We always try to take-off and land into wind. If the wind is from the west, we take-off towards the west on runway 27, if possible. Having a headwind of 20 knots means that we start with 20 knots on the airspeed indicator and it takes less time and less runway to get up to flying speed. It's the same on landing, in a 20-knot wind we stop on the runway with 20 knots of airspeed having used less runway than if it were calm.

A wind from the side, a cross-wind, makes directional control more difficult and therefore limits are set on how much crosswind is permitted. If the wind exceeds the limit we use a different runway, or different airport. These limits can be a bit arbitrary but we dare not get caught exceeding them. Similarly, it is often permissible to take-off and land with a tailwind, but the limit is only a few knots, 5 or 10.

Once an aeroplane is flying, from within seconds after take-off until touchdown, the wind has no effect on how it flies and requires no control correction. It does affect navigation of course and unexpected strong winds have carried aircraft many miles off course and several have never been seen again. The problem was that, in the old days, pilots had no idea what the wind might be. After you leave the ground there was no way of measuring the wind so pilots were depending on a weatherman's vague guess of the wind strength high above an empty desert or ocean. Weathermen sometimes guessed wrongly, and pilots got lost. They could not see or measure the relative motion between the ground and the airmass.

That was true right up until my time. My first jet had a Doppler-effect based radio that bounced radio beams off the surface and calculated our groundspeed and drift angle, knowing which we could calculate the wind direction and strength. The Inertial and SatNav equipment fitted to modern aircraft calculates precisely where on the planet it is, and precisely its groundspeed and direction, relative to that spot. If the aircraft computers know both airspeed and groundspeed they can calculate the wind's speed and direction at that spot. I have flown in a jetstream wind of almost 240 mph over northern Canada and it was quite smooth, and even during turns we felt no unusual effects or airspeed variations whatsoever.

Towards the end of a flight, when the passengers are expecting to be on the ground in a minute or two, it can be quite alarming when the throttles are opened, the nose of the plane rears up and it climbs away. It can be several minutes before you get an explanation, or you might not get one at all.

The pilot has just done a go-around (that's American for overshoot) and it is a busy time. He has to ram the throttles fully forward, raise the gear (American) raise the flaps in stages, tell Air Traffic Control, follow a prescribed procedure and plan ahead for his next move. So, sorry if you weren't told. The reason, more often than not at busy airports, is that the aircraft ahead did not vacate the runway in time either because ATC brought you in too close behind, or the one ahead missed his turnoff. Or it could be that your pilot was a little too high or a little fast to land, or the weather was not good enough to allow a clear sight of the runway, caused maybe by a squall of wind and rain.

It is not an emergency procedure or a problem or in any way dangerous—just the safer of two options in the circumstances. Normally the pilot will ask for a quick circuit round to try again.

At the end of a flight, after applying the parking brake, the engines are shut down, leaving the APU running for electrics and air conditioning. The Captain will fill in the Tech Log noting any faults found during the flight and remaining quantities of fuel and engine oil, and then he signs it. Only then is the flight complete.

Chapter 4
Joining BEA

Graduating from Hamble led almost automatically to a job in either BEA or BOAC. In College we were asked to fill in a form detailing which airline, aircraft and base we would prefer. When the job offers came, our entire course was taken by BEA and allocated to the Trident airliner based at London Heathrow. So much for choice.

The Trident had three engines, three electrical systems, three hydraulic systems, three autopilots, three pitot and static ports for air instruments, three separate sources for the radio guidance to feed the autopilots, and—oh yes—three pilots. The goal was to achieve fully automatic fail-safe approach and landing in adverse weather, particularly fog (remember the dreadful fog/smog problems of the fifties and sixties?). The idea of having three of everything was that, even if something failed in a bad way, the other two could overcome it, or outvote it in the case of an autopilot fault. It should be obvious which system had the fault as it would be the odd one out.

I started this, my first Proper Job, in November 1973 as a second officer with one stripe and, I have to say, a decent salary although we had to pay back to the company a portion of our training costs from that salary, either spread over five years or in a lump sum if you resigned. I was so proud of my new BEA Pilot's uniform that I wore it for my wedding the following summer. The airline business was set up on a seniority system which greatly discouraged mobility.

You didn't change companies for better pay, as you would have started again at the bottom, so we tended to stick with the same company throughout our career. As we became more senior we had more stripes on our sleeve, salary rose with each year's service, prospects for promotion increased (but we still had to pass the course) and we could reasonably expect to retire on the top salary from a fleet we really wanted.

My whole Hamble course started the same day, all on the Trident, and training could not cope with us all at once and so they organised us into small groups spread over the next six months. Groundschool on the Trident was detailed and lengthy as it was a complex aeroplane and they went into far too much detail, poring over wiring diagrams at times. I suppose we knew it thoroughly in the end. The design called for three pilots, a Captain who sat in the left seat and two co-pilots who took turns in the right seat (P2) or the third seat (P3 or systems panel operator).

The rear panel for P3 had all the fuel, electrical and hydraulic system controls, many auxiliary systems plus panels full of fuses and circuit breakers on the rear wall of the cockpit. Later aircraft types replaced all fuses with circuit breakers to protect equipment. Modern houses now use circuit breakers too but, instead of maybe ten, aircraft have many hundreds, all listed in a book if you know where to look.

Learning to fly the Trident followed right after passing the groundschool exams. It involved session after gruelling session in the simulator, each session lasting four hours, with two hours preparation before, and a debriefing after. First, we get used to flying a fifty-ton trijet, the fastest airliner there was—quite a step up from a Cherokee or even a Baron. Then we slow it down and get to feel out the stall, first nibbling the edges where the stick shaker starts to vibrate the control columns, commanding us to push the nose down, open the throttles and level the wings. In the event that both pilots were really clueless and kept pulling, there was a mechanical stick pusher that pushed the nose down for us.

Having learned how to get into trouble, and out again, we practised instrument flying and landing procedures with three engines, two engines and occasionally on just one engine. One great advantage of the Trident layout, three engines grouped together at the rear, is that when one engine failed there was little swing caused by asymmetric thrust. Push on a little rudder with the correct foot and it was fixed. Much simulator time was spent with an engine failed. Then we learned how to program the autopilot to land itself—a unique trick in those days. Finally we had to take an aeroplane away for days to a quiet airport to practise landings, as the simulators of the day were not good enough.

The Trident simulator's visual, what the pilot sees projected on his window, was the product of a small camera moving over a large board painted with a landscape and a runway. The last few hundred feet of the approach looked quite unrealistic, so for total realism we flew a real Trident round and round the circuit at Prestwick, first on three engines, then on two.

The Trident's undercarriage was notably unforgiving. It had sturdy main legs, with a wheel on each side, and two tyres on each wheel, but the significant characteristic was a very short oleo travel. There was very little spring travel to cushion our arrivals. When the training Captain signed off our landing practice, that completed our licensing requirements as fully qualified Trident co-pilots employed by BA. I had made it across the river to solid ground, though all the other pilots were higher up the riverbank than me.

Nowadays pilots start life with two stripes, to reassure passengers who might worry when the Captain goes to the loo. New pilots in my day started with a single stripe on our uniform jackets, and it took a couple of years to earn the second stripe. But at least there were three of us. I found the three-pilot environment was good for training, and for starting in the industry, because it gave the brand-new pilot somebody to copy. The captain was too old, high and mighty (this was the mid-seventies remember) but the new pilot could model his behaviour, flying standards and indeed attitude to authority, on the senior experienced co-pilot.

Having learned how to handle a Trident, and all kinds of emergencies, in the simulator and on base flying, we then learn the regular airline pilot job while carrying passengers during Line training. On the Trident this meant flying with a senior Training Captain and a senior copilot who between them dragged us up the steep learning curve that shaped us into useful airline pilots. It was around this time that British Airways (BA) was formed by merging BEA and BOAC.

For the first few flights the senior co-pilot would accompany the new chap on the external check. The walkaround is usually started from below the entry door, at the foot of the stairway down, and we walk around the aeroplane in a clockwise direction checking everything in sight. We check the nosewheel, the tyres, steering connections, the sliding oleo, the safety downlock pin must be removed, the retract bay is clear.

We walk back out to the fuselage side and check that the small air holes that connect to the instruments are clear and clean, check the radar dome on the nose is secure and intact, and so on. The official list goes on for pages but you get the idea. We walk the perimeter, along the front of the wing, round the tip and down the rear of the wing, then forward under the wing to inspect the main undercarriage, back and around the tail and so on round to finish where we started, at the steps back up to the main door.

Among many other things we were advised on how to address the passengers on the cabin address. We were told to be ourselves, keep it warm and friendly, truthful and informative but not technical. Use simple words and expressions, but avoid emotive words that might be misconstrued. For example a pilot might say, "We are presently encountering hurricane-force headwinds at our cruising level, so I am afraid that we will not reach our destination on schedule." Now imagine some foreign passengers with "leetle eenglish," or an elderly couple hard of hearing.

The little old man grabs the hands of his little old deaf wife and yells, "Martha, better start prayin' hard. The Captain says he is afraid! There's a hurricane where we're goin' and we might not make it."

Life on the Trident

After passing the conversion course for the Trident we had recurring checks every six months when we had a great deal of practice in the simulator, including all the faults that could go wrong on autolands or normal operations. The rest of the time we flew it all over Europe, from Iceland to Israel. But most flights were exactly the same. Take off, airways flying to a radar approach to an ILS, land on a strip of concrete, taxi to a concrete and glass building, an hour later do the same thing back to Heathrow. Almost every flight involved either a take-off or landing at our home base at Heathrow.

The Air Traffic Controllers at Heathrow were superb, the best in the world, but the airport management and London politicians imposed a stupid "noise abatement" procedure on departing Tridents, which entailed reducing power at a critical phase during take-off to tiptoe past the noise meters installed at several points around the airport.

Smoking was allowed in those days and it was awful. Not many pilots smoked and very few smoked on the flight deck, but when one did, on a long flight, I said I was off to the toilet and didn't return for a while. If they lit up again I needed the toilet again. Thank goodness it was later banned, for comfort and safety.

In the seventies British Airways had a large department dedicated to air safety. They produced a monthly publication whose title I forget as we called it the 'Horror Comic.' Inside were details of (usually) a major accident involving another airline from which we could learn valuable lessons, plus every major or minor incident involving any BA aircraft for that month, grouped by aircraft type. I always read all of the Trident reports, generally just a handful of minor failures. I was interested to read how they had been dealt with plus any remedial action by engineering or management that could prevent a recurrence.

I also skimmed through the other aircraft types for any interesting events, any lessons that applied universally. One thing that impressed me was that there were pages and pages detailing every engine shutdown on the Boeing 747 fleet. In those days our 747 aircraft were powered by Pratt and Whitney's big fan engines, and they regularly threw turbines blades causing vibration, high temperatures, some thrust loss and the resulting shutdowns.

The Trident was the only airliner in the world that could autoland in fog, the so-called blind landing system. Decision height was as low as 12 feet, whereas everyone else used 200 feet, at which point they had to see the approach lights and runway touchdown zone lights. At 12 feet we need see only one runway light such was the confidence that the correct bit of runway would be under the wheels at touchdown. The captain was always in charge for autolands.

He briefed the co-pilot to fly a nice steady approach down to 12 feet, then call "Decide" and if the Captain failed to call "Land" P2 would call "Overshoot," open the throttles and go, assisted by the Captain and P3. When the Captain 'saw the light' and called "Land" he took control for the auto-touchdown, called for P2 to apply reverse thrust, and applied the toe-brakes while keeping the aircraft on the centreline. At 80 knots he disengaged the autopilot and manually steered onto the taxiways.

It all worked out beautifully and our main problem was convincing ATC that we could land in the conditions. Typically we would be given the weather and told to expect a long weather delay. We would tell them our limits, and after a bit of consultation and confirmation the controller would clear us down early and slip us below the holding stack into the approach pattern. Our big problems really started when the weather improved to Boeing levels, then everybody wanted in.

But it was years and years before the Americans caught up, first with the Lockheed L1011 TriStar and eventually the Boeings. The trouble was that we could perform our miracles only at airports with the Cat 3 ground equipment and that meant London, Glasgow, Edinburgh, Manchester and Belfast, plus maybe one or two places in Europe. My training covered the Trident 1C and the long range 2E version. Another group of pilots were trained for the stretched Trident 3B version.

As new co-pilots we were teamed with a very experienced co-pilot for some time (a lesson learned from the Staines crash). In good weather, on a two-sector day (flight there and back) the Captain would fly one and give the other away, on a three-sector day it would be one landing each, and if we flew four sectors we had one each and one for the autopilot, an autoland just for practice. The P3 did the paperwork, read the checklists, operated the systems panel, and watched the other two for errors.

The happiest times generally involved getting off the plane somewhere abroad for a nightstop. One of my first was in Athens in March 1975. We landed at the old Athens Hellenikon airport near the city and at that time of year stayed in the luxurious Hilton hotel. In the summer months we used the Apollon Palace Hotel, on the beach at Kavouri. The large bathroom of my Hilton room was lined entirely with marble, but unlike Lord Elgin I didn't try to remove any.

I made acquaintance with my first bidet, a fabled European extravagance. I tested the taps, and sure enough water started to gush into the bowl. When I moved the middle lever, the water was instead directed to a sprinkler in the bottom of the bowl, from which it shot up to the ceiling, spread out and rained down, soaking me and the rest of the bathroom. I tidied up, showered, changed into smart civvies and was late meeting the crew in the penthouse bar.

The next day was a standover day during which I explored the Plaka district and the Acropolis. I remember that visitors were allowed actually inside the Parthenon building on the Acropolis, so this was just before the preservationists and health and safety put up barriers that seem to move further out each visit. We all had dinner in a rustic barn of a place, where we ate barbecued lamb chops washed down with either retsina (vile stuff) or Demestica.

On a trip to Agadir, Morocco, the company bought us lunch in a restaurant so we ordered steak. The waiter looked Moroccan but sounded French so I ordered mine very, very well done, the other two said medium. Mine was very pink but acceptable, their steaks were still twitching and were sent back to be cooked. Cyprus was always fun as food was very cheap and wine and brandy sours (a happy combination of the three cheapest liquids in Cyprus, brandy, lemon squash and soda water) were even cheaper. Meze is a speciality of Cyprus where they just keep bringing little snack dishes, all kinds of tasty treats, until you beg them to stop. We often went to rustic restaurants where Petros the proprietor would rearrange his tables, and other customers, to accommodate a big table for the British Airways crew.

Other places where food and drink were expensive were not so much fun, because of the allowances system. Our crew hotels were booked room-only, and the company paid us cash money based on the cost of typical meals (no booze) in the overnight hotel. So we took the money to a local hostelry where it covered a good meal and some wine as well. Some places (expensive places) some crew members (especially cabin crew) kept the money to take home, stayed in their room, and spent as little as possible. They lived on sandwiches and snack-pots brought out in their suitcases, known as "Delsey dining," after the popular luggage manufacturer.

On some trips because of the scheduled timings we had a couple of evening hours, then a whole day off, and left early next morning (almost 35 hours off), called a standover. On such a Stockholm standover, one stewardess stayed in her room while the rest of the crew explored the city, and found a sex shop on the high street (unheard of on UK high streets in those days, but Swedes were broad minded). The rest of the cabin crew put together and bought her a toy, a plastic moulding with a natural shape and batteries that made it vibrate.

On the flight home the chief steward slipped it into her bag and at London was first into Customs to ask them to, "Look in the blond girl's bag for something embarrassing." When the whole crew were assembled, the Customs man obliged, asked to see in this girl's bag, as he was always entitled to do, and pulled out a vibrator, and then a second vibrator, looking round the crew as if to ask, "Who carries two?"

One of the perks of working for an airline was the ability to impress one's friends by having them in the cockpit during a flight. One school friend had booked BA to Bucharest and I arranged to fly his return flight. The Captain gave me the sector so I flew him in the flight deck's fourth seat all the way back to London. The main perk was the cheap travel. We could go to the Staff Travel office and buy tickets to anywhere on the network at a fraction of the advertised cost, but we were standby. We were boarded after everyone else if there were seats left. If not, try the next flight.

I bought tickets for my wife and me to Kenya, and booked a good hotel, full board. On our first morning we were awoken early by a noise that sounded like very heavy rain on the trees outside. "I suppose we can expect the odd heavy shower in the tropics!" I said, hoping it would stop before we headed off to breakfast. But on opening the heavy curtains, the view from our balcony was of a beautiful sunrise, with golden sunlight from the Indian Ocean filtering through the baobab and palm trees, whose leaves chittered in the breeze, sounding like rain.

Everything seemed cheap in Kenya, the hotels and the drinks. In fact the beer was much cheaper than the orange juice because, I discovered, beer prices were government regulated but hotels could charge as they pleased for OJ. There were several other guests our age in the hotel, all airline staff, while most other guests were much older. Kenya was a bit exclusive in those days. We arranged a short holiday in Jersey at the end of that long hot summer, and it poured with rain the whole time, but we couldn't even use the shower because of the summer-long drought.

On the news we heard about the tragic mid-air collision of a DC9 and a British Airways Trident over Zagreb on its way to Istanbul. I phoned my parents in Glasgow to reassure them that I was not on board, as for all they knew I could have been.

British Airways management seemed scared of the unions then, especially the Transport union which controlled all the ground staff and the cabin crew. I remember stories about cabin crew helping out passengers with some extra service, and being disciplined (fined) by their union for helping because it was outside their industrial agreement. Heathrow became tagged as "Thief-row" in some tabloid papers because there was so much alleged pilfering and management did nothing for many years. Once when I flew as a passenger to Heathrow I borrowed a large suitcase from my parents but forgot to ask for the key.

There was nothing of value, just everyday clothes, so I left it unlocked but when I pulled it off the luggage belt it was locked, both sides. Why could that be? I had to ask the baggage services office for sets of spare keys to unlock it.

There were so many restrictive practices, and downright skiving, but management would not rock the boat as they knew the Union would pull out an essential segment of the workforce, effectively closing down the whole Heathrow operation. Losing one day's revenue plus the resulting loss of confidence was too big a risk, and the union played on their fears. On many occasions, when arriving at Heathrow there was a lack of support staff. We needed a whole array of staff each with his own job, including staff to position the steps, buses with drivers to transfer the passengers, loaders to unload the bags, a ground engineer, and so on.

All were under the direction of a redcap who supervised the operation on the ground and switched on the guidance system when applicable. Nobody was allowed, in the heavily unionised environment, to do anybody else's job. The one exception was pilots. Several times, when arriving on a stand where the steps were a few yards away but there was nobody to push them, the other co-pilot and I opened the hatch in the cockpit that led down to the equipment bay. We dropped down inside, opened the hatch from the equipment bay to the outside, dropped onto the apron and positioned the steps ourselves. And that was tolerated.

One night in Geneva we discovered that the Swiss were holding a national holiday, Swiss national day or whatever, the lake shore road was closed to traffic and the Swiss uncharacteristically let their hair down and had fun with fair grounds, comic apparel and silly toys, topped off by a display by the Red Arrows (their first season with the then new red Hawks), followed by a phenomenal firework display over the lake.

In 1977 I made a serious mistake. I took my wife on a long trip to Cyprus. In the cockpit with me were Captain Chatfield and Andy the other co-pilot, a single chap. In the cabin were four cabin crew, a chief steward and three attractive girls. We hardly spoke on the way there, and had two separate taxis to the hotel, but we arranged to meet in the bar early that evening. The Captain and Andy were early and the rest of us arrived more or less together. It took Capt. Chatfield a second for a head count and he swiftly ordered 8 brandy sours.

My wife Anne didn't drink, but took the proffered glass anyway and decided it was really quite nice. Somewhat later that evening (2 or 3 brandy sours & some wine later) we were all seated around a big dinner table for meze, with the Captain sat one end, chief steward at other end and I sat in the middle of one side, with my wife on my left next to the chief steward who turned out to be gay. She had never come across someone openly gay before, so that was an awkward novelty. On my right was a stewardess, while Andy sat opposite me with a girl on each side.

Another brandy sour and a few bottles of wine into the meal, opposite me Andy was busily snogging with one stewardess while the other girl, who was to be married a couple of months later, sat between him and the Captain. Beside me was the third girl, who was being very friendly with a hand on my thigh and trying to snog me. Yes, while my wife was seated at my other side chatting to the gay chief. Meanwhile a little Cypriot guy with a guitar entertained us, playing and singing a selection that included John Denver's Annie's Song. Anne and I later reminisced about the trip in general, the singer, and in particular that song, which became 'our song.'

Next day we hired a car and the Captain (who had once been based on the island with the RAF) drove us around the sights in the Paphos area and up to Mount Olympus. It transpired that Andy had slept with the girl he was snogging at dinner and she was with us in the crowded car. That day the girl who had tried to snog me at dinner found another target and spent that night with him. By the time we went home my wife had acquired a totally wrong impression of what went on during nightstops. "This is a one-off, never happened before, honest!" but would she listen?

Later, I took her on a Stockholm standover trip which redressed the balance a little as nothing went on. We socialised to some extent, one beer in the Captain's room, went for a meal, a boat trip round the city canals, but definitely no hanky-panky. THIS is a normal trip, I kept stressing. But she never let me forget that Cyprus trip.

I took my wife on another interesting and unusual trip, to Inverness. Because of some strange quirk of scheduling, the three pilots arrived late on the Friday night and departed Inverness early on the Monday (I've no idea where the cabin crew went). I took my wife on such a trip and early on the Saturday we hired a new Lada saloon from a company called "Sharpe's Reliable Wrecks." He had started with old low-mileage second hand cars before buying the new Ladas, and was very cheap. We drove from Inverness, west and north through the wild Highland scenery.

I had lived in Surrey for a few years by then and become used to the manic cut-and-thrust traffic conditions in the south-east, so I stopped occasionally to take a photo of a lonely glen with the narrow road stretching miles into the distance with not a single vehicle in sight. The Mercury Hotel was very helpful. They transferred our Saturday night booking to their west coast Ullapool branch, so that we stayed for the whole weekend free of charge. On the Sunday we found an alternative road back to Inverness and handed back the car, having enjoyed a great short break. I remember one Captain who regularly took two empty suitcases on these long Inverness trips, and went home with them full of goods to sell in an antique shop in Surrey.

Anne and I both took part in sporting activities, starting with badminton classes in the local secondary school, and the badminton club in the primary school where my wife taught. Later I arranged regular meetings with other badminton players, doubles with three chief stewards in British Airways, singles with Roy, a pilot on my course, and mixed doubles with other people my wife and I had met at the classes or clubs. There was also a badminton club in a hall in the country park near our house. I had to give it up after several years due to tennis elbow. Other social activities included dinners at the Model Aircraft club where I was an enthusiastic member, and dinner parties with friends in British Airways or Anne's work.

Then there was the school badminton club's cheese and wine party. On the last evening before the Christmas break we all took some wine, glasses and snacks to the school hall. I had a game of badminton (always mixed doubles), then a generous glass of wine during my off-court time and a snack. When it was my turn to play again I found that I couldn't hit the shuttlecock. I was always a fraction of a second behind it.

I felt absolutely normal and unaffected and would have driven home quite confidently at that stage, but my coordination had suffered badly. I have never had a drink before driving, not even one, since that night. However my wife Anne didn't drink but did drive, so I had a few more glasses and the evening finished very sociably in the nearby house of one of the club members.

1978 was an Eventful Year. On March 12th we set off for Hamburg with me sitting P3. It was a normal take-off, with the Captain handling, the co-pilot called the usual, "V1-rotate," the Captain pulled back to lift the nose into a climb. When the altimeter and vertical speed indicator agree that we have left the ground and climbing, the co-pilot calls, "Positive climb," the captain replies, "Gear up," actioned by the co-pilot. As third pilot I watch to see that everything is called and executed correctly.

After the undercarriage was selected up on this occasion, we heard the usual noises—thump, thump-thump, thump. "Hey, there shouldn't be four!" I thought. I glanced around the gauges, "Engine failure!"

We all agreed it was number three (the main clue was, it wasn't turning) so the Captain called for the shutdown drill on number three, actioned by the co-pilot with me watching, and ready to break his arm if he tried to shut down the wrong one. We flew back to Heathrow and landed normally, they gave us the spare aeroplane, transferred all passengers, meals and bags and we set off again, without incident.

On the brighter side, later that year on a Glasgow nightstop I happened to contact Donald, the friend who had been my best man, and he just happened to have a spare ticket to a concert in the city by the Corries folk group. That was a lucky day. I often used Glasgow nightstops to meet up with my relatives or school friends.

Then we learned the importance of the airspeed indicator check on take-off. The non-handling pilot always called 80 knots, and if the pilot handling the taking off agreed, we continued. On this occasion he disagreed and called "STOP!" and we aborted the take-off. Since one of the airspeed indicators is wrong, and we're not sure which, we certainly don't want to go flying.

A couple of days later it was my turn to do the landing at Heathrow so the Captain flew the approach but the flap wouldn't come down so I had to land unusually fast, but there was plenty runway to slow down using reverse, without overheating the wheelbrakes. Then, in October, engine number 1 gradually failed during the climb towards Geneva. We watched it a bit then shut it down and returned to Heathrow: no drama. I was in the right seat that time.

I remember a Moscow trip in winter, with poor weather forecast and a handful of passengers booked (about 9) and I thought "Just cancel and we'll all go home." What we'd nowadays call a no-brainer. But no, one of the passengers was a "Queen's Messenger" carrying a diplomatic bag containing, I expect, the Queen's messages. For political reasons we could not cancel the flight so off we went, with plenty of fuel to mess around at Moscow and then divert to Helsinki in Finland, our guaranteed good weather alternate. And that is how it turned out. We saw not a glimpse of Moscow's runway, flew to Helsinki where no passengers wanted to get off so we refuelled and brought everybody, and the Queen's messages, back to Heathrow. We had a long gruelling day, almost 8 hours flying, and wasted tons and tons of fuel.

In lighter news that year, the unusual flight timings gave us a few hours of free time in Gibraltar this day while another crew took over the plane, and we were allocated one hotel room and a couple of taxis. The Captain and other co-pilot plus a couple of cabin crew arranged to make up a four at bridge in the hotel, so that left Sonia, Margo and me to do some sightseeing. I don't know who had the idea (Margo probably) but our taxi dropped us at the foot of the cable car that took tourists up to the top of the Rock.

We clambered on board a full cable car and were stuck in the middle with scarcely a view out, but once at the top the scenery, the views of the tiny scrap of land that is Gibraltar, with Spain on one side and the Straits on the other, were inspiring. We also made distant acquaintance with some of the apes on the rock and headed for the cable car down to where our taxi would be waiting. This time the cable car was empty, except for the three of us. The scenery, with views all around and down, through all that un-obscured Perspex, was breath-taking, but we became aware that Sonia was standing holding the pole in the centre of the car with clenched fists and eyes closed. She looked frightened. We told her, "Nothing to worry about, nothing can go wrong, never has, never will." But still she looked tense. To take her mind off her fears I cheekily undid the top button of her uniform blouse. Then after the stroke of a finger inside, I undid another one.

Far from objecting, she went for my shirt buttons, with Margo's encouragement. To cut a long story short, in a little while I had undone all her blouse buttons, and she had undone all my shirt buttons, the cabin support forgotten. Margo meanwhile had undone my trousers, which were now round my ankles, and I unhooked Sonia's bra. A glance around revealed that we were less than a minute from the bottom station. That time was spent in frantic buttoning, zipping and bra adjustment, so we were properly uniformed, and maybe a little flushed of face, as we walked to the taxi.

Nor was that the end of the story. Back at the airport Margo asked to borrow some money for bargains in the duty-free shop. Sonia couldn't help so I lent Margo the cash, to be repaid on the flight home. But on the way home Margo came into the cockpit, where I was third pilot, and whispered confidentially that she didn't have enough cash on board to repay me, "but after the flight come back to my place and I will give it to you there!" A loaded sentence if ever I heard one. I insisted that she borrow money from the bridge players and sort it out with them and the cashier back at base. I mean, a frolic in a cable car is one thing, but I had a wife at home.

That still isn't the end of the story, as a few weeks later while parked during a turnaround in Marseille in a Trident 1C Sonia took me aside and explained that she had told the two gay stewards in the rear cabin about our romp in the cable car, and had told them we were to consummate the encounter in the rear toilets that day. Would I play along and wind them up? Wondering what Sonia might have in mind in the confines of the toilets, I agreed. I hadn't mentioned the cable car to the other crew, or anybody. You're the first person I have told. Honestly. The Trident 1C was unusual in that the partition between the two rear toilets was designed to be easily taken down.

The plan was to go into separate toilets, remove the partition and squeeze past each other into the other toilet, and then after a convincing interval replace the partition and emerge from the other door, making it obvious that we had been 'together.' Unfortunately the ruse failed as without a proper screwdriver the partition would not budge. That really was the end of the story, as Sonia later remarried and I never saw her again, while a couple of years later Margo was tragically killed when a Viscount in which she was a passenger was shot down in Rhodesia (now Zimbabwe) by terrorists using a shoulder-launched missile. It barely made the news at the time. That was the second in Rhodesia that year. There were far too many innocent civilian airliners being shot down over the years for my liking, by all sorts of people, later including the Russian Airforce and US Navy.

Those jolly incidents between the pilots and cabin crew were very rare. One that didn't happen, but might have, was outbound on a Cyprus standover when the chief steward took our meal order and asked, "any other requests?"

The Captain jokingly asked if the stewardess could serve the meals topless (there was a rumour to this effect going round, involving the well-endowed Sonia as it happens). The steward said that (stdss A) had a better figure but Hilary would be more fun. She certainly had a fun smile and a glint in her eye, but the reason I remember her was that for the whole 3-day trip she teased me about how young I looked. I was 28 but "could pass for 21!"

So the next time I had almost 3 weeks away from work I grew a beard. Instead of splitting my leave into two separate weeks as I usually did, this time I took two consecutive weeks with three fixed days off at each end, and we used it to move house with all the attendant cleaning and DIY.

One amusing incident involved two friends, two of the senior cabin crew with whom I regularly played badminton. They were fond of practical jokes, so when Frank saw some vintage mint condition model cars on display in a very seedy Cypriot bar, he told his friend Tony, an avid collector who used to scour the markets and bazaars of every far-flung destination for Corgi, Matchbox and especially the older Dinky models. The bar in question was the entry point for the brothel upstairs.

Frank neglected to mention this, but he did say that the manager did not realise that these models had any value and would probably bin them when the place was to close and be demolished within a few weeks. So our hapless friend wangled a Cyprus nightstop and was seen banging on the door of the bar before opening time, shouting through the letter-box, "I want to see your Dinkys!"

My wife and I visited the doctor with a very personal problem, no babies after many months of trying, so he sent us to family planning. On our last visit to them before we were married the priority had been for us both to keep working to pay the mortgage, and we had been told that pregnancy could occur at any time of the month barring a few safe days, so she was prescribed the pill. But this time a different story emerged.

Yes it may be possible to get pregnant anytime, but you are likely to get pregnant on only an optimum day or two in the monthly cycle. Back home a quick check on the calendar revealed that last month I was in Inverness, month before Stockholm, before that Cyprus, and so on. Being a jet-setting airline pilot can bring up unexpected problems. Family planning involved more planning than we envisaged, and daily thermometer readings. However a year or so later our first gorgeous little baby daughter was born.

Months before that expected arrival, I had taken my wife on a short holiday to a resort near Athens, to the very hotel which I always enjoyed when I stayed there with the crew, the Apollon Palace in Kavouri. We enjoyed exploring the little seaside resort, the local restaurants, and it was a short and very cheap bus ride into the city centre where we explored the usual tourist sites.

We saw Syntagma square, the Acropolis, the funicular ride to St George's Mount, and so on. It was a few weeks later when we moved house and I grew my full beard. We were supposed to ask management permission, but I neglected to do so, maybe in case it didn't grow properly. Afterwards nobody said a thing so I kept quiet, and kept it neatly trimmed.

It had been a long night, starting at noon the previous day when my wife decided she needed to get to the maternity ward. All night I stayed with her, and around breakfast time I got to hold the most beautiful baby ever. Then the hospital told me their visiting times and threw me out. I drove home, stopping to buy a pack of wide pink ribbon which I tied with big bows around the two Scots Pine trees in front of the house. Fathers had no rights to paternity leave or anything else in those days, so I phoned British Airways to tell them sorry, in my exhausted and euphoric state, I was in no condition to fly a Trident that afternoon, and hung up. I also phoned our relatives with the news and went to bed for a few hours.

On one of those nightstops in the Apollon Palace, the whole crew went for a meal then to a nearby nightclub as we had a late pick-up. The aircraft wasn't due in until lunchtime so we had a few drinks and a fun time, but while walking back to the hotel the other co-pilot said, "I hope it is good weather tomorrow and it all goes smoothly."

The captain tempted fate with, "You shouldn't say that, Sod's Law says we'll get an aeroplane with no autopilot and have to hand fly all the way home." And sure enough, it came to pass. It was no problem on take-off and climb out, but at high altitude jet airliners become very sensitive on controls and it took great concentration to maintain height and heading precisely. The Captain and I took it in turns to fly manually. Jet airliners are very, very rarely hand-flown in high altitude cruise, for good reason.

The old Athens Hellenikon airport (closed 2001) could be tricky occasionally, if the wind was blowing the wrong way. Usually we flew a standard ILS approach to runway 33, as the prevailing wind came from the west or north-west. But in a strong south-easterly we had to pick our way from a beacon on the offshore islands directly towards the city centre then, when really close and fairly low, a visual right turn took us along the coast towards runway 15. The new Athens airport (Eleftherios Venizelos) has no such problems, just a long drive into the city.

Nice in the south of France is similar, in that runway 04 is used whenever possible as the approach is over the sea, and a sharp right turn after take-off to miss the hills is not a problem. But if the wind is from the south the approach takes a lot more care and skill. It needs a visual circuit and a tight left turn between the hill and the town to line up on runway 22. The old Gothenburg Torslanda airport had a hill at each end which made life interesting, but Landvetter is a great improvement.

The old Oslo airport, Fornebu, was right on the seaward edge of the city and had an interesting approach low over the city, but operations moved in 1998 to a big new airport on an old ex-military airbase and the city is expanding towards the old airport, which is now scarcely discernible. The new one is so far out of the city that I fell asleep in the crew bus every time.

The prize for the most difficult airport on the Trident network has to belong to Gibraltar. There is a huge lump of rock standing sentinel over the Atlantic's entrance to the Mediterranean, connected by a narrow isthmus to mainland Spain. The British outpost of Gibraltar consists of the rock, with its habitable fringe on the west side at sea level, and part of the isthmus. The runway has been built across the isthmus and extended west into the bay on a causeway.

The border with Spain lies a few hundred yards north of the runway, and the airport occupies most of that. The road to the border crosses the middle of the runway, and is obviously closed when aircraft are due. Part of the pilot's problem here is the shortness of the runway, as at each end there is sea, a wall, then runway with no over-run area. There is nowhere to put the aerials for radio guidance (ILS) so we depend on Precision Approach Radar (talk-down) and seeing the rock to avoid it.

The main problems in Gibraltar however are the wind, and the Spanish, who in the old, pre-EU days, occasionally used to threaten to shoot down anything British in their airspace. When the wind blows from the southern half of the compass the rock creates massive turbulence in its wake, and that has serious effects on even fast heavy jets arriving and departing. Flights can be badly affected by the wind, or cancelled altogether if the wind exceeds certain laid-down limits.

I set off as co-pilot on such a day (I made no record of which day) and when contacting ATC at destination we copied the wind reports for runway 27's landing end, the far end and top-of-the-rock winds. They were all within limits, just. The Captain always did the landing at Gib, so I flew the cruise and descent, having discussed actions in the event that the wind went above limits. If the wind was above limits or we just didn't feel comfortable we would go up and away, with a hard left turn after passing the rock and before encroaching on Spanish airspace.

We saw the runway, and the rock, from miles away and dropped the flaps and wheels early so the checks were finished a long way out and we were cleared to land. The Captain took control early to get the feel of it and flew perfectly down the PAR approach path, with me on throttles giving him power adjustments up and down as requested in the turbulence. Wind reports from Tower were still just within limits.

As we came into the lee of the rock we were thrown about considerably by the turbulence, and at a few hundred feet above the water we encountered a downdraught of rapidly sinking air, carrying the aircraft down with it towards the water. The Captain called "Full Power," I rammed the throttles fully forward to the stops, and our descent became more controlled but still downwards. At least now it was gently downwards, and towards the runway, not the water. With the touchdown zone of the runway looming right in front of us the Captain announced that he would land after all, called "idle thrust," levelled off above the runway calling for "Full reverse!" and flared for a reasonable landing.

So I went from full power forward, idle for a second or two and straight to full reverse as we hit the runway. That, together with a bit of braking, allowed us to turn off the runway before the road crossing. Within a few seconds we had gone from a normal approach to a dive towards the water, to a full power go-around, to a landing and short rollout with the passengers probably none the wiser and unaware of the drama and adrenaline flowing in the cockpit. That was probably the closest I ever came to a serious incident. It was a great piece of flying by the Captain.

One of the certification requirements for an airliner is that if a window or door blows out at very high altitude, it has to get down to breathable atmosphere within a specified time, and we were told that was why the aircraft was certified to allow use of reverse thrust while flying.

Loss of pressurisation never happened so the desperate dive was not needed, though we often practised in the simulator. We routinely selected reverse idle in the flare on short wet runways but very rarely was reverse needed in the air, not unless we were asked for a demonstration of the Trident's second unique trick (the first one being autoland).

I was on a trip back to Heathrow from Dublin, late at night, traffic was quiet. We called London ATC early and asked for a straight-in on the easterly runway (in use at the time) but were told to expect a hold at Ockham away to the south of Heathrow. "Strange with so little traffic about. Are they closed? Is there a secret security alert?" we wondered among ourselves. We complied of course, aiming to reach the holding beacon at 9000 feet and 210 knots. When we were really close to Heathrow, and still high and fast, ATC asked if we still wanted a straight-in.

The cabin crew were already happy and prepared (as we had briefed on the possibility) so without hesitation we accepted, I pushed the nose way down to increase airspeed and at the same time pulled the airbrake lever and reverse, to achieve a phenomenal rate of descent. The rate of descent was off the clock and the altimeter hands a blur, but for less than a minute, all it took to lose over ten thousand feet. Then I dialled the speed back to raise the nose which brought the descent rate back on the scale with the speed reducing to approach speed while still maintaining a rapid descent. That is just not possible on other jets—you either reduce speed OR you descend. You can't go down and slow down.

Within a minute or two of admittedly hectic activity, we were down in the approach slot, on the centreline, on the descent profile and back at normal approach speed, with reverse cancelled, airbrake in, dropping flaps and landing gear and bringing the throttles up to approach power. The Trident was the only airliner that could do it and it was very rarely used. I am quite certain that those Controllers had a bet on about whether or not we would accept the challenge, and could achieve it.

Even without resorting to using reverse thrust the Trident was remarkably versatile. I remember flying one approach for Captain Ian Banks early in my career, and I messed it up. We were too high, away above the correct approach path, and I apologised in advance for what I expected to develop into an embarrassing go-around and second attempt. But Captain Banks had said, "We can see the airport over the nose, so we can make it. Have faith, hang on in there!" And sure enough I managed to coax the old Trident down into the landing slot and he made a perfect landing out of a very untidy approach.

Though the Trident was really good at coming down, it wasn't so hot at climbing, especially the mark 1C. At certain airports the Trident 1C normally had to circle the airport, sometimes twice, to gain height before heading north across the Alps. In hot countries they all suffered when heavily loaded, and it was jokingly said that they climbed only thanks to the curvature of the earth. A Lufthansa pilot, observing the climb-out of a Trident 3 from summertime Malta, echoed this on the radio saying, "It is just as vell the vorld is round, Bealine!"

That may be my first evidence of the German sense of humour. There was another, if heavy irony counts. Sometime later when British Airways had a pilot surplus, some BA co-pilots were loaned to Lufthansa to cover their pilot shortage. One of these was called Fred, a tall, gangly and untidy individual sometimes referred to as 'the unmade bed.' Fred reported that, after overhearing some attempted banter on the radio on the approach to Zurich, his Lufthansa Captain leaned over and confided, "You know Fred, zees Sviss, zey haf no sense of humour!"

Some shorthaul co-pilots were also seconded from Tridents to the VC10 fleet, resulting in an illustration of the quite different eating habits of longhaul and shorthaul pilots. The VC10 steward brought in the Captain's meal, then the co-pilot's and engineer's. The Captain unrolled his napkin, removing the cutlery and laying it out around his plate, fork on the left, knife right, spoon above. Then he tucked the cloth napkin into his collar to keep his shirt spotless. He took the little individual salt and pepper containers and sprinkled some pepper over his beef, and some salt on the potatoes. He sniffed the delicious aroma from the first-class meal and observed appreciatively, "This looks delicious!"

Just at that the ex-Trident co-pilot handed his empty tray back to the engineer and remarked, "Yes, mine was!"

In the late nineteen-seventies British Airways set up an experimental service based on an American model and called it the Shuttle service, which operated from London Heathrow to and from the main UK cities Glasgow, Edinburgh, Belfast and Manchester. The idea was that flights would be scheduled to operate every hour, passengers would not book but would be guaranteed a seat if they arrived more than 10 minutes ahead of departure time. The revolutionary bit was that, in case the scheduled flight filled up, an additional aircraft with crew would be standing by to fulfil the guaranteed seat promise. This back-up aeroplane would be a Trident 1C and I would often be one of the pilots sitting on instant readiness waiting for the phone to ring, the tingle of excitement, the brief announcement "Squadron scramble!"

Oh no, that was the Battle of Britain. We would be told, "Glasgow Backup, parked on A3," and the effect was the same as we rushed to our aircraft just outside the standby room. If the scheduled service filled up early it would depart early. Occasionally, when the scheduled flight was nearly full and the deadline was approaching, we would be sent out to prepare our aeroplane just in case we were needed.

One of the reasons for Shuttle was that, previously, businessmen travelling back and forward for a meeting would ask their secretaries to book them a seat on each of five or six return flights from 3 pm until the last one at 8, as they didn't know when the meeting would end. The result was that all the flights would soon show as fully booked, but on the day there were so many no-show passengers that no flight left full and the last couple had few passengers. No doubt passengers who had been told we were full were lost to competitors.

Tickets not used were refunded, cost the businessmen nothing, but BA lost money. For the passengers the Shuttle meant just turning up and boarding. Most passengers on business travel light, but suitcases could be taken to the gate, right beside the aeroplane, and sent down a chute directly to the loaders, greatly reducing the chance of lost baggage. Only the Belfast flights had significant security procedures in those days. Passengers could pay their fares on board, but there was no catering because of uncertain numbers and possible delays.

For the pilots on backup duty it meant days of waiting around at London or one of the four destinations, which all needed spare aircraft and crews. I started reading much more than hitherto, novels and military history—or combinations of the two like C.S. Forester, Nigel Tranter or Spike Milligan. At Heathrow I also practised conversation with women. The newly set up Shuttle office was staffed by a selection of attractive young women, and a couple of men that I hardly noticed.

We never saw any other Heathrow ground-staff for more than a minute or two a month, but Shuttle was different. On arrival we checked in with them and were told which flights were likely to require a backup, and to which outpost we would probably be sent overnight to provide morning coverage next day. Rather than just go to sleep or read in a chair, I sometimes stuck around to chat if they weren't busy, and became friendly with several of them.

One beautiful and charming lady in particular, whom I'll call Elaine, used to chat with me once or twice a week. I knew nothing would come of it of course as I was married, with a baby, and she was attached, but when Elaine threw a party she invited me, with my wife, and one or two other pilots. And when my wife and I had a big party we invited a couple of Shuttle girls, including Elaine of course.

My wife and I were invited to a themed party by my buddy Mick and his wife Karen who lived nearby. Mick and I had been on the same course at Hamble and we had been firm friends ever since. The party theme was "one garment only," and there was much speculation as to what garment the guests would choose. As it was wintertime, overcoats were essential, but they came off at the door to reveal some interesting choices. One imaginative guest had to pop upstairs to change, into a cardboard box, with head and arm holes. It didn't look the most comfortable of evening wear.

The meet and greet party opening the door to arrivals had the additional duty of checking guests for additional unapproved garments, like panties, which when found led to a rising chant of "Off, Off, Off, Off!" and off they came. I wore a boiler suit which was terribly boring of me. A kilt would have been much more comfortable (as it was warm in there) and interesting (especially for the ladies in England I later discovered), but I did not have one at the time. But the star dresser of the evening was the extrovert David who wore only a black tie. It was a very long and wide black tie with an elastic retainer around his waist. With care, that was just enough to be decent in carefully posed photos but left nothing to the imagination.

For my first six years on Trident the rostering department produced the flying roster in monthly blocks, and published it two weeks before the start. They shared out the work evenly so that each pilot had about the same amount of flying days, standby duty and days off, and a similar mix of long and short trips. However BOAC then used a different system called Bidline, which was used by the big American airlines. British Airways decided to implement the BOAC system on other fleets, including ours.

The Bidline system is too complex to explain, but can you imagine a family of twelve children whose mother prepares dinner for them each day? The mother cooks enough food for herself and all the children, and selects her own food during preparation. Then she lays on a buffet dinner with a great variety of food, maybe a couple of steaks, some roast pork, a chicken curry, and so on. At dinner time the eldest child is handed a plate and let in first to the buffet to select what he wants—say the bigger steak, the gratin potatoes and sautéed mushrooms. Then the second child helps himself to the buffet, and so on down to the youngest who is left with toad in the hole and boiled cabbage—every day.

As you might guess from my bitter description, I was one of the junior pilots who were put on standby duty every month, for the whole month, apart from three fixed days off, and that went on for ten months. A typical day might be home standby from 6 am. then a phone call at 8 am. inviting me to standby in the airport crew room instead. I'd sit there for a few hours and then be called to operate the afternoon Brussels-and-back to replace a chap whose car had broken down. On my return I would be given duty times for the next day, usually standby, occasionally a trip they already know is uncovered, maybe even a day off. It is a rather unstable lifestyle.

Our training up to this point had emphasised the doctrine that if all three engines' instrument indications were not the same, if the three pointers were not lined up parallel, we should call "STOP" if below V1, or "Engine Failure" if above. But in March 1982 I became aware of an exception, on the occasion when I was assigned during a block of standby for a special ferry flight. The Captain was in Management or Training, and he explained that we were to bring back from Stuttgart a Trident 2 with a damaged engine, so that the engineers could replace it using all the splendid facilities of the hangar at Heathrow.

The normal rules stated that we must be able to continue safely even if an engine failed, and they still applied. But in this case we would be down to our one lonely remaining engine to sustain us on the lift-off, climbout, and subsequent landing. Much time was spent checking that our operation complied with the figures sent by the aircraft manufacturer.

The aircraft was loaded with enough fuel to get to London, with an alternate and a safety margin, but no cabin crew, and no galley equipment that could easily be removed. The Captain did the flying, of course, aided by two alert copilots. With luck, and two good engines, we made it to Heathrow without incident. In due course I received a commemorative dark blue tie embroidered in white with a three-pronged spear, with fire emanating from only two of the prongs.

A couple of months after that experience, the cure for my unstable lifestyle was discovered, and turned out to be another aspect of the American Bidline. On months when there was less work than usual the American airlines would keep the senior people working to maximum capacity, and lay off the juniors without pay. But since British Airways was a state-owned airline and we had a strong Union, we were laid off on basic pay. That was what the foreseeable future held, since we experienced a downturn in the airline business, and our fleet was being run down as the Tridents were old by then, they had high fuel consumption, and the Americans were beginning to catch up with autoland technology in bad weather. So I sat at home for a few months, but the timing could not have been better as our second gorgeous baby daughter had just been born and I could be a full time dad for a while.

Chapter 5
Flying the Cabin

Management decided that unemployed pilots could fill in doing other jobs elsewhere in the company, but took their time deciding where. Job offers elsewhere in British Airways eventually arrived, following long negotiations with all the Unions involved. Many of us elected to work as cabin crew as it kept us airborne, out of the tedium of office work and out of rush-hour traffic. Along with a few colleagues I elected to work from the Gatwick base where most work involved day-trips, rather than long-haul which could involve regular two-week trips away from the family. From Gatwick, BA operated both scheduled and charter flights using Boeing 737 and wide-bodied TriStar aircraft.

The pilot group joined a big bunch of girls, most of whom had been trolley-dollies with Dan Air, Court Line, Laker or other less well-known charter airlines. The regular cabin crew referred to us as Nigels, a generic name for pilots apparently. One lovely girl had been a policewoman but had given it up in disgust after being beaten up by a thug on a busy high street in daytime, somewhere in Sussex, where not a single member of the public tried to intervene or offer help.

The cabin crew force at Gatwick consisted of a core of full-time crew who worked all year round, supplemented in the busy summer period by temps taken on for six months each year. They were promised that if they came up to standard they would be considered first next year, and maybe get a permanent contract after a couple of years. Their basic salary was a little better than they were used to, but when their Union rep delivered the presentation describing all the allowances, bar commission, overtime payments and additional bonus payments, they were surprised and delighted. As overpaid pilots we didn't attend the presentation, and we didn't get the commission, bonus or overtime payments, just our basic.

Our induction course covered serving drinks and meals, sell, sell, sell the duty frees, and of course all the safety equipment and procedures which were the cabin crew's principal responsibility according to the CAA. A typical flight started with a briefing by the chief steward or stewardess, then check the safety equipment, check that all the bar, meal and duty-free trolleys were present before the passengers arrived. The charter flights were generally full and it was a rush to get everyone on board and seated, but we had more time to be helpful on quieter scheduled flights. Once the doors closed and we started moving, the designated person read through the cabin address and safety briefing while the rest of us did the pointing, smiling and life jacket demo.

The flight itself comprised a bar trolley with a free drink for everyone, a new set of trolleys with a hot meal, then the duty-free trolleys. On shorter flights, like those to Spain, it was hectic, but on longer services to the eastern Med we had the same work pattern but much more time and could fit in extra smiles and an extra round of drinks. What can I say about these day-return trips? You fly there, you fly back.

There was not much sexual harassment on these flights, but I did once have my bum pinched by a lady with a few empty gin miniatures on her tray and another Nigel reported the offer of a quickie in the loo. On one TriStar trip the chief steward was very friendly, but just for the first half hour. Then the girl sharing my trolley told me she'd just informed the chief, "He's a Nigel!" Then we each came to realise, "Oh, he's one of Them." On TriStar I liked to work the under-floor galley, on the deck below the passengers.

That is where the trolleys were stowed, leaving much more room for seats on the main deck, and it was reached using a couple of electric lifts (or elevators as it was an American airplane). I enjoyed the challenge of handling dozens of heavy trolleys and having each one in the right place at the right time. It occurred to me that on longer flights it would be a good place for a dalliance, to join the mile-high club. I heard that there used to be a steward who thought the same, and tried to lure the girls down with tales of finding the "golden rivet."

The girls at Gatwick were young and energetic, and even after a day's work were keen for a night out, in a local restaurant or bar with their workmates. Once after a TriStar trip they asked if I wanted to go along, yes even though they knew I was a Nigel, but I declined. "Don't be a boring old fart, come along, it'll be fun," pleaded my 22-year-old workmate for the day. But I knew that's just what I really was, and went home.

The occasional trans-Atlantic charter flight cropped up on the TriStar. The first was a Saturday afternoon departure to Toronto. I picked up Trisha, a gorgeous looking blond stewardess who lived nearby, and drove her to Gatwick in my Lotus. The flight was uneventful and we arrived early evening. This was our first nightstop abroad and the night was young, so a steward and myself went with Trisha and another girl into town and up the CN tower, the world's tallest free-standing structure and tallest tower at the time. We ate in the revolving restaurant and dared to walk on the glass floor (1100 ft above the street, straight down), and then danced in the nightclub further up in the doughnut.

When that closed in the early hours we took a taxi back to the hotel totally exhausted, and grateful to be ignored by the girls. Next morning we had arranged to meet early for breakfast and take a trip to nearby Niagara Falls. My alarm woke me early, I stumbled to the bathroom and glanced in the mirror then went back to bed. Niagara would still be falling next time I visited, I decided. We took the evening flight back to Gatwick and I drove Trisha home in my Lotus. I never did get back to visit the Falls on a nightstop.

The next was such an unusual trip that I went to great lengths to take my wife Anne along. I asked my parents to come from Glasgow to look after our two little girls, I contacted the Captain to ask if my wife could sit on the extra cockpit jumpseat, and I bought her a staff ticket. It was to be our only chance of a summer holiday together that year so better make the most of it. Incidentally, I think I also had notions of working in the galley down below and taking her to see "the golden rivet," but somebody beat me to the galley job. I was assigned to work closely with a girl I'll call Elaine, on opposite ends of the same trolley.

On the Tuesday we filled up with 393 happy holiday makers and flew them off to Bangor in Maine, the quiet north east corner of the USA where crew and passengers quickly cleared US Customs and Immigration. Another crew took them on to destination, as that would have taken us over the permitted duty time so we were off to a local hotel for two nights. On the Wednesday we hired a minibus which the Captain drove, taking us on a sightseeing tour to the beach near Bar Harbour and then back again.

After almost 48 hours off, Thursday was a flight to Los Angeles, where we all disembarked into a bus straight to our hotel, avoiding a two-hour queue as we had already cleared US Customs and Immigration at Bangor (a cunning plan). After an hour or two at the crew party in the Captain's room, I slipped off for an intimate and romantic dinner in Pancho Villa's, the Mexican Restaurant in the penthouse of the neighbouring hotel, with Anne. (That's my wife, OK, not a stewardess, pay attention).

Our hotel was the plush Sheraton Miramar in the fashionable Santa Monica district of Los Angeles. The Miramar hotel, and Santa Monica in general, have regularly featured in locally made movies, in the nearby suburb Hollywood. On the Friday we walked around the streets, shops, beach and pier of Santa Monica. Saturday saw us doing the Universal Studios tour along with a few others from our crew. We saw all the usual sights, the Jaws shark, the earthquake, the flash flood and the Psycho house, that everyone knows now, but back then it was all novelty.

A year or so earlier our friends in the Aldershot model aeroplane club had emigrated to California, and I bought their Lotus Elan+2 S130. It was white with a glittery silver roof and went like the wind, on a clear road. I loved that car, can you tell? Our Sunday in LA was spent visiting these émigré friends, who had replaced the Lotus with a locally bought and restored Porsche. An old Porsche, which was really a VW Beetle in a tarted up bodyshell, and it sounded and drove like an old Beetle. Not a patch on a Lotus (please don't tell Graham I said so).

Monday, let's see, Disneyland. How could we visit LA and not have a day in Disneyland? We saw Mickey and all his friends, we saw the sternwheel steamer, Old Thunder railroad, the fairy-tale castle and the model Matterhorn bordered on one side by a monorail and submarines (well it's Disneyland).

Another Tuesday (is that a week already?) was spent in shops in Santa Monica buying things to take home for our girls, then a bit of a sleep as I will be up all night watching the passengers sleep. We don't need to stop for fuel going east, with the perpetual tailwind. We arrived home Wednesday lunchtime. That was an unusual trip, not many like that come up.

Although I was very occasionally aware of a liaison between a member of cabin crew and a pilot, the cabin crew tended not to date pilots as a rule. One exception to the rule was the stewardess with whom I worked on that long trip to Bangor and LA. At the crew party in the Captain's room on the first night in LA Elaine had lingered, I discovered, to the very end and spent the night with him. Later, while we worked together on the same trolley, I discovered in casual conversation that she was attracted to Captains in particular and had scored a few others. I met a couple of other girls like her, but only when I was a steward or co-pilot.

Another US trip was rostered, again with a stop at Bangor, Maine. Gatwick crews liked a good time, and we didn't get many opportunities, so we were all picked up in several cars for a steakhouse that somebody knew about. They expected us and we were shown to "the big British Airways table" and handed menus. You can have steak. We each ordered a steak, and a drink. After a short time a waiter came to say the steaks will take a little while but he had a tray of complimentary snacks to nibble while we waited. Thanks very much! Five minutes later another tray of different snacks arrived, "to nibble on while you're waiting." Then another tray.

By the time the main course arrived we were full of snacks, and the steaks were enormous, sagging over the sides of the plates. Each would have fed a family for a weekend. A long weekend! We can leave the fries but felt obliged to make some kind of impression on the steaks. My steak-knife hacked a slice off the well-done side of mine, and I managed that. None of us managed more than a fraction of the meal. I had been looking around the steakhouse and noticed that most customers used doggy bags to take the remnants, OK most of the steak, home. But some stalwarts manfully chomped their way through a whole steak with grim determination. They were the ones whose ample behinds were sagging over the sides of their chairs.

When the bill came it was accompanied by a cake, decorated with sparklers, and iced with the message "Welcome British Airways Crew." That was a friendly gesture but more food was the last thing we needed. The next afternoon we flew off on the next incoming charter flight to Orlando, Florida. The following day after breakfast in a typical American diner, the crew went to the aptly named "Wet & Wild" theme park and we got wet having a wild time on the flumes, slides and "Banzai Boggans." There was nothing we wouldn't try, even the vertical drop. In the evening we went to Rosie O'Grady's, a lively Western bar with entertainment, in town.

During that spring I pined for a bit of hands-on flying at the British Airways flying club at Wycombe Air Park (Booker) where I hired a Cherokee for a check flight. After that I was allowed to take one away, with friends on board, and did so several times. I took friends to a model aeroplane show at Sywell, I took a model club friend and his son for a flight over their house, and I took a couple of friends for a flight out west, destination Thruxton. I asked in the flying club, "Where's the phone to call Thruxton for their weather?"

The instructor looked at me, and after a pause said, "Look out the window, it's a lovely day!" I could tell he thought I was being a pedantic twat, over-professional, so we piled into the Cherokee and set off for Thruxton. When we were within hailing distance I called up for the weather report and was told, "Thick fog, can't see a thing here."

Right then, I thought, I will plan a diversion, turned towards where I thought Blackbushe must be and called them up. The weather there was fine, but when I looked back at my map I had a shock! I can't believe it, I'm LOST! Nothing out there matches where we ought to be on the map. I tuned in one VOR and took a bearing, changed to another VOR, plotted the second bearing and where they crossed! Smack over Aldermaston prohibited area. I dipped a wing, "Yes, that's it down there. What height is prohibited? Below 2400 feet, and we are at? 3000 feet! That's a relief." The stop at Blackbushe was interesting and the flight back to Booker uneventful.

While serving as a cabin steward at Gatwick we were not given any leave in the summer, but I had a two-week block of leave in November. On the Monday I stripped the wallpaper in the hall, and on the Tuesday morning I had a phone call. It's British Airways, "to let you know you are down for a TriStar course at Cranebank on Thursday this week." I already flew on TriStar in the galley, what are they on about?

"What sort of course do you mean exactly?" I asked.

"You are on a pilot's course, to fly as P2 out of Heathrow. You did put it down as your first choice in the annual bid." That was almost a year ago.

"Oh, so I did. OK then, 9 am Thursday at Cranebank," then to my wife, "We need a painter/decorator, fast! Nice of them to give me two days' notice and cancel the rest of my leave."

The pilots who had been flying the Trident 3B before our redeployment were put back there, but my fleet was being run down and was still over-crewed so I had been given my choice of fleets. Those in a similar position took up flying jobs all over the airline.

Several of my course-mates had not relished the idea of being redeployed in the first place and so instead had left BA to seek flying jobs elsewhere, while others left to start new businesses or go full time on a business side-line they had already started. On the other hand, one or two liked their redeployed job so much that they never returned to flying. Over the years our course also lost one friend to a flying accident while flying his own glider. Rumour had it that one went to jail (and so out of BA) for assaulting someone with a baseball bat in a domestic altercation. One of our number who did go back to flying had to stop flying due to stress. It just became too much for him. We had all been on Tridents before this break but, when recalled to flying afterwards, Hamble Course 721 was scattered all over the place.

1. I first flew solo in a DHC1 Chipmunk like this. The college at Hamble had used them when first set up, but after changing to more modern Cherokees they kept this example and a couple of others for spinning practice.

2. Here is the Cherokee 180 in which I flew my first solo at Hamble. They were nice modern aircraft, with a nosewheel and a heater, but lacked the miniature-fighter charm of the Chipmunk.

3. The Beechcraft Baron was a flying E-type Jag, a powerful fast glamorous machine.

4. The revolutionary Hawker Siddeley Trident was very fast and the only aircraft with autoland-capable triple autopilots. This shot, showing the first British Airways colour scheme, was taken at a very wet Glasgow Airport in December 1979, by Lewis Grant who kindly allowed me to use it, along with a couple of his other photos.

5. BEA introduced the Trident airliner in 1964, and this example has been preserved by the Duxford Aviation Society in BEA's 1964 colours.

6. The Trident cockpit, cutting edge technology of its day, now looks dated. In the centre is a rolling Doppler map display.

7. This is a composite panorama of the ceiling to floor systems panel. The third pilot, P3, or systems panel operator, was a fully qualified pilot who looked after this lot. His seat was on rails so that he could either be right behind the other two pilots, monitoring takeoff and landing, or he could slide aft and right a little to operate the systems panel.

8. The Trident's roof panel had oxygen masks for the pilots, lots of light switches, anti-icing controls, and the three big coloured levers were for hydraulic systems.

9. The droop lever seen here is the one that caused the crash at Staines in 1972 when it was raised at too low a speed. By the time I joined, a lock had been fitted that prevented its movement until the flaps were up.

10. A family photo with my father and mother, wife, Anne, and two little girls, Rona and Sheena, in front of the Lockheed Tristar that I flew as copilot at the time. This was on the apron at Larnaca, Cyprus, on the way home from a family holiday.

11. I took my wife on a trip to Cairo with a couple of free days, and of course we visited the pyramids and (if you look closely) the Sphinx.

12. For something completely different, I came back to Glasgow to fly the 1950s style HS748, affectionately known as the Budgie in British Airways. It had two RR Dart turboprops and manually deployed airstairs to the rear door.

13. After a year I finally made it to the Budgie's left seat, the best job ever.

14. My first trip on the 747 after training was to Hong Kong. Here a Boeing 747 is negotiating the tricky chequerboard turn at the old Kai Tak airport. In good weather and daylight the hills are easily seen. A great photo by Tony Li.

15. In this shot, from a different vantage point, an aircraft very low over the Kowloon rooftops about to complete the turn. Many thanks for the photos to Tony Li who was at senior school in Hong Kong at the time.

16. The Boeing 757 was the first big jet that I flew as Captain. I carried passengers right from the first flight, but I already had 2000 hours left seat flying, and had flown the big 747-436. I flew this particular aircraft often on the Glasgow to JFK New York run. This photo at Glasgow by Lewis Grant.

17. The cockpit of a Boeing 757, taken by a visitor who later sent on the photos.

18. Another Lewis Grant shot, this time a Boeing 767 on final approach to Edinburgh. This controversial 'World Images' colour scheme was introduced in 1997 and featured fin designs from around the world.

19. My whole crew about to board the crew bus for my last flight, from Entebbe in Uganda to London England

20. There I am in the front cockpit taxying out for a joyride in a WW2 trainer, the SNJ6 Texan, a better thrill ride than anything by Disney or Universal.

21. My first flight in a floatplane, at Jack Brown's seaplane base in Florida. Instructor Maurice on the float, preparing to hand-start the engine.

22. A memento of our holiday in Barra, taken by Captain Bill Wells who flew us home. A second Twin Otter is touching down on the sand in the distance.

23. The highlight of my post-retirement trip was this flight in a helicopter, whose rotor blade is top centre, up close to Mount Cook in New Zealand.

24. Another highlight, there were several, was a flight in this Cessna floatplane with a lady pilot over Mount Tarawera, from Lake Rotorua.

25. The great city of Sydney from the front right seat of a Beaver floatplane.

26. And this is Now. A recent photo of Captain Anne Anderson in the very modern cockpit of a Boeing 787 Dreamliner complete with head up displays, flying into the sunset over Canada.

27. For this small aerobatic model I also designed flying skis, stabilised by a tail.

28. Touchdown of a fast flying-boat with a foreplane airbrake, a bit different.

29. And here is my jet design, JayTee, on a slow pass with take-off flap

30. The low wing version JayLow is a little more sporty.

31. And we're back to Tridents. Here is the world's only flyable Trident, a radio controlled twentieth scale version that I designed, built and flew, powered by a single miniature jet turbine engine.

Chapter 6
TriStar

It was great news of course, getting back to flying, ending a year and a half of reduced income and the uncertainty as to whether or not my career might continue. And the TriStar flew an interesting mixture of short flights around Europe and longhaul flights to USA, middle east, far east and east Africa. It was also a very modern aircraft with loads of electronics and as good autoland capability in bad visibility as the Trident, and I was already familiar with the galley and coffee makers.

The TriStar, or Lockheed L1011, was another trijet but this one was wide-bodied with 3 big fan engines, the Rolls Royce RB211, one in the tail and one under each wing. It had been ordered originally by BEA for European operations and had been flown (even after the merger) with three pilots. As in the Trident the two co-pilots had alternated in the P2 and P3 seats. However by this time some longer range versions had been bought and the old BOAC management got their way and changed it to a longhaul operation with a Captain, a co-pilot P2, and a Flight Engineer in the third seat. It made sense for longhaul.

The systems panel was more automated than the Trident's P3 panel, but Flight Engineers contrived to make it look complicated. And Flight Engineers monopolised the Tech Log, showing it only to the Captain when necessary for approval and signature. One or two flight engineers handled the Tech Log like Gollum with the One True Ring ("My Precious").

Having a Flight Engineer suited me, as I had double the amount of flying and next to no technical worries. My opinion on technical problems was irrelevant as the Captain had an expert who knew the answer or could find it in the book. The engineer also did all the paperwork, and liaison with cabin crew, and ate the third most popular crew meal. Already the Flight Engineer was an endangered species though, as new aircraft being introduced, like the latest version Boeing

747 and MD11, had done away with the third crew member and operated with a crew of just the two pilots.

While on the groundschool course, one of the novelties was our introduction to HF radios in preparation for longhaul flying. These were used on long range flights across oceans, jungles and deserts. We were told how to select a suitable frequency from the available range, depending on time of day and distance to the target radio station, and we were told to shout a lot and persevere. We were also told that within a year or two they would be obsolete as VHF satcom became widely available. But when I retired over twenty years later we were still shouting over HF radios.

For all its auto-sophistication, the TriStar was still an old-style aircraft, and our conversion course was of the old style with a lecturer, a blackboard, notes and books. We learned all about the aircraft and its systems, passed the exams and then flew the simulator until we could handle any emergency. Since this trijet had an engine below each wing, when one of them failed there was considerable swing towards the dead engine, requiring a bootful of rudder the other way to keep straight, but we became used to handling that.

When an engine failed the pilot or engineer spotting it just called "Engine Failure" without specifying which, just in case the first impression called was wrong. Then both pilots and the engineer had to agree which one had failed before calling for the appropriate shutdown drill. The training people had another trick up their sleeves though. The flight engineer made the usual calls, for a simulator trip, of "V1, Rotate" and "Engine Failure!" but this time there was no swing, so having pulled as usual on 'Rotate,' which rudder do we push?

Then the real problem became apparent when the stick shaker warned of a dangerously low airspeed. The nose was way up, pushed up by the low-slung wing engines without the nose-down counteraction of the high centre engine, the one that had failed. OK guys, point taken. We don't just pull, we aim for a specific nose-up angle and hold it, regardless.

When I say the TriStar was old-style, it had individual round dials for instruments, artificial horizon in the centre with compass below, altimeter right and airspeed left. The vertical speed (very important) was below the altimeter. All of these had to be scanned constantly when instrument flying by hand. The engine instruments were also individual round dials, three sets for three engines, on the centre panel straight ahead of the three throttles. Just to polish off our training we each had three circuits in a real, but empty, aeroplane at some quiet airport (Prestwick). The first was on three engines, then a second circuit was on two engines with a go-around, then another circuit on two to land.

Landing this beast was different from previous aircraft as we sat so far above the wheels. Add extra height from the nose-up tilt on approach and it was impossible to judge the wheel height above the runway so we had a radio altimeter which bounced a signal off the runway between the main-wheels to measure the height accurately. We raised the nose and closed the throttles in accordance with the engineer's height calls of 30, 20, 10.

On landing, you need to be below 100 feet and above 50 feet as you pass over the start of the runway (threshold). So the sequence should be 100 feet call, pass over the threshold markings, 50 feet call, and 30, 20, 10 into the landing flare. If 50 feet is called before, or 100 feet is called after the threshold, we go-around.

At Hamble we had been taught to land in a cross-wind by kicking off drift at the last second before touch-down, and this same technique was used on the Trident. We would fly the final approach with the nose pointed, not straight at the runway, but off towards the windward side. The technique was then to flare normally, but still pointing at the runway edge, and push on the rudder to line the aeroplane up with the runway the second before it touched down. Getting the timing just right was quite difficult. Push the rudder too late and you have landed with sideload on the wheels. Too early and the aircraft starts drifting with the wind towards the runway's downwind edge.

The Tristar autopilot was programmed to handle cross-winds differently. It still flew down the approach with drift offset into wind obviously, but at 300 feet it applied rudder to remove the drift so that the aeroplane was pointing straight down the runway. At the same time it lowered the wing on the side from which the wind was coming so that the aeroplane side-slipped into wind, to ensure that it still tracked the runway centreline.

Thus, if for example the wind was blowing from the right, all down the approach the runway was off to the left in the window, the nose was pointed to the right of the runway. At 300 feet the autopilot applied left rudder and dipped the right wing (using aileron) and held that position with so-called crossed controls right through the landing flare. So the right wheel landed first, followed by the left wheel, and then the nose was lowered, all the while with some right aileron applied.

We were encouraged to use this same technique for manual cross-wind landings, but we waited until we were down to maybe 150 feet. Then a bit of downwind rudder to cancel the drift and dip the into wind wing with aileron, flare and hold the aileron into wind for the rollout. I found cross-wind landings so much easier using this technique, since timing was no longer critical, and used it on Tristar and all twin engined aircraft since. It could not be used on four engined aeroplanes in case the dipped wing scraped the outer engine on the runway.

The really interesting bit that followed was the line training. The first trip was via Kuwait to Dubai, where I learned something new. You know the Monopoly square called GO, upon passing which they give you £200? Well Dubai was like GO. It was the place with the highest meal allowances on the network. Another thing, we met in the hotel bar in 'happy hour' and ordered, "Four pints of Tartan please, eh barman!" Nearly called him Jimmy out of habit; it was like being back in Glasgow on Shuttle.

The price doubled after happy hour so we headed for the Intercontinental Hotel, where happy hour was an hour later, followed by a restaurant. Dubai has been redeveloped so much since then that I could not recognise it now, and it's even more expensive I'm told. The TriStar flew to many other places in the Middle East including Jeddah and Dammam in Saudi, Bahrain, Abu Dhabi, Doha and I visited them all but just occasionally.

In all these places the meal allowances paid to us in local currency amounted to significant sums, so we often took the money into town and ate local, for two reasons. One was to save money, and the other was we felt safer eating what the locals ate rather than their interpretation of European dishes. Once when I ordered lasagne in a plush hotel it was still frozen deep inside. I developed a taste for the local 'fast food,' sold at countless stalls all over the market area.

A Shawarma is made by alternately stacking meat and additional flavouring on a spit. The meat was roasted slowly on all sides as the spit rotates in front of a flame for hours, and some meat was shaved off fresh in view of the customer, and wrapped in pita bread together with vegetables and dressing, just like the Turkish kebab now familiar in Europe.

My final training trip, my check flight, was from Heathrow to Abu Dhabi, Dubai, Bahrain and via Bombay finally to Bangkok. By that time I had passed, or thought I had, but the old Flight Engineer Mike White said the final stage was a visit to the Patpong, or red-light district of Bangkok where he took us to a bar where friendly young Thai hostesses came over to us and asked us to buy them a drink, while scantily clad girls danced on stage. It reminded me of saloon scenes in old westerns, with just the costumes changed.

We went from there to a nightclub where we sat watching the stage. I sat furthest from the stage fortunately, as some naked Thai girls danced and performed tricks with bananas and ping-pong balls, aiming them towards our drinks. Very, eh, educational Mike. Did I pass? In the Patpong next day I bought a couple of mounted oil paintings, production line stuff for tourists, but quite emotive in their way, and hanging on my walls to this day.

Here I was, finished my training and a regular line pilot on the Bidline, right near the bottom. Bidline had been changed for the better by this time. Instead of permanent standby, junior pilots like me were now on the trips nobody wanted like Cairo and Khartoum, with some Eastern USA nightstops and European day trips thrown in. I went to Khartoum in Sudan every month, and stayed in the Hilton Hotel, right at the meeting of the Blue Nile flowing from Ethiopia and the White Nile from Lake Victoria, Uganda. Don't believe the descriptive names, they are different shades of muddy brown.

The Sudan had just become a strictly Moslem country and no alcohol was available (like Lenzie where I grew up). It did rather dampen the crew's social life though. We played Trivial Pursuits and other sober games, and watched television, but still no skinny dipping or spin the bottle. Hotel television was weird. What we watched wasn't Sudanese, it was programs and movies taped from the BBC and ITV and brought over, so we sat in the middle of Africa watching old British movies and TV shows inset with adverts for Woolworths and trailers for Benny Hill on Thames TV.

About that time I had bought a Sinclair Spectrum Plus computer, the later version with half decent keyboard, and my friend Brian introduced me to a word processing application that started me writing my first book, Basic Aeronautics for Modellers. Strictly speaking I had started writing by hand when I was on Trident permanent standby, but hand-writing was hopeless and I had given up. Word processing was so much better, as I discovered when my Spectrum was plugged in to the television in Khartoum.

I wrote there regularly and within less than three years had virtually completed the book. The text was word-processed almost entirely in the Khartoum Hilton, while the multitude of diagrams were hand-drawn in Cairo and other places without Spectrum-friendly televisions.

The TriStar was fitted with a system called GPWS (Ground Proximity Warning System) which made a "whoop, whoop" sound then said in a dull American voice "Terrain, Pull Up, Pull Up" about 20 seconds before it predicted we would hit the ground. That's not the time to discuss the issue, it needs an immediate and automatic response of full power and pull up, and that's what we were trained for. There is an apocryphal story of a South American crew approaching Madrid whose last words on the voice recorder were, "Shut up, gringo!" (in Spanish) in response to "Terrain, Terrain, Pull Up, Pull Up." It's probably not true, but it's definitely the wrong response when given 20 seconds to live.

The device did indeed save lives though. A crew trying to land a Boeing 747 at Nairobi were warned by GPWS, responded correctly, and later discovered that due to the wander of the inertial nav systems, and lack of radio update, they were over a Game Park, not the airport. The GPWS equipment became nicknamed the Game Park Warning System.

In those days BA flew several times a week to Cairo, and on three days it went on to Khartoum. The Friday flight stopped there, the Sunday one went on to Dar es Salaam in Tanzania, and the Tuesday flight went on to Mauritius. The crew in Khartoum who took over the flight to Dar, down on the coast, waited there on the ground for a few hours and then flew back to Khartoum—known as a Dar shuttle. The crew taking over the weekly flight to Mauritius had a whole week off in Mauritius waiting for the next aeroplane in. That, coupled with the two or three days in Khartoum on each stopover extended the trip to two weeks, a long time to be away from the family.

Cabin crew were rostered, and two kinds were found in Mauritius. The grumpy ones had been caught off standby and hated a two-week trip with minimal allowances and a suitcase of inappropriate clothing. The happy ones had requested the trip along with their pals for a free holiday on a tropical paradise in the Indian Ocean and had packed sunscreen and their water-sports and beach gear.

The Airline had a new computer program for fuel calculations, known by the acronym SWORD. It calculated the minimum amount of fuel that would be needed to complete your flight, on a good day, and gave rise to the saying, "he who lives by the sword will die by the sword." There was much management emphasis on carrying SWORD fuel, no more, but most Captains would play safe and add a bit extra, just in case.

On my first trip to Khartoum, we had a day off and were then to operate the Dar shuttle, starting in darkness in the wee small hours. Company rules stated that we had to pack our bags, clear the room and take our luggage with us on these there-and-back flights. I tried to get a good sleep beforehand but was woken by a strange noise and smell. Looking outside I could see a dust storm, stirred up by a fresh wind, and the smell was the fine desert dust infiltrating the room. In the reduced visibility I could no longer see across the Nile, and going back to bed I was kept awake by the worry that I would be given the return flight back from Dar and would have to decide how much extra fuel to carry, just in case.

In only twenty minutes the view across the Nile became clear again, I decided thirty minutes extra fuel would do, and I went to sleep. In the event I was given the flight south to Dar where the weather was clear enough for a visual circuit. During the long turn round we all sat in first class and watched a movie on the entertainment system and then flew back in daylight to Khartoum, with magnificent views flying past permanently snow-capped Mount Kilimanjaro, the highest point in Africa at almost 20,000 feet.

The Captain had surprised me by loading SWORD minimum fuel so that when Khartoum ATC reported a dust storm in progress on our arrival, we flew once round the hold then diverted to our alternate Jeddah, in Saudi Arabia. We had been gone less than ten minutes when Khartoum called after us announcing that the wind and dust were settling, but we were committed. Returning then would have left us completely stuck if the dust returned or the runway became blocked. In Jeddah the weather was guaranteed perfect and there were three runways to choose from.

After a night or two in a plush hotel where we had been given a wad of valuable allowances, we flew home arriving a day early. So the Captain was smarter than I first thought, or maybe he was subtly making a point to management about the wisdom of minimum SWORD fuel.

It is in the nature of the job, the whole airline industry, that some of the staff have to be working on weekends, bank holidays, and even Christmas and New Year. The Heathrow ground workers were different in those days (maybe still are) because much of their weekend and holiday work was covered by overtime that they graciously agreed to work. But aircrew were contractually obliged so my first New Year on TriStar was spent in Cairo. We went down to the hotel bar party to bring in the Egyptian New Year, then later we adjourned to the Captain's room to bring in the British New Year, and we had the whole day off to recover.

The way the schedules worked we sometimes had two whole days off in Cairo, making it a four-day trip, which was ideal for taking family members. I took my wife on one of those, joining the crew party the first night, then next day we spoke to the hotel concierge and arranged a taxi, an air-conditioned Mercedes, to take us round the sights for the day. We had pre-arranged a price for the trip but of course our guide included a stop at his brother's shop and his cousin's market stall. But we saw the pyramids at Saqqarah, the ancient ruins at Memphis (no, not Elvis) and the pyramids and Sphinx at Giza.

The pyramids at Saqqarah are among the oldest in Egypt, and here we hired a guide to take us down inside, through some very cramped, claustrophobic and deserted passages. My wife whispered, "Can we trust this guy? We could get mugged." But it was a bit late to ask when deep inside the pyramid. We encountered no mugged tourists, and eventually returned to the sunshine.

It was mid-summer at this time, and blazing hot outside, so when offered a guided tour on horseback or on foot around the desert area surrounding the more popular pyramids at Giza and the crowded Sphinx, we declined. I spotted an alternative, a one horsepower two-wheeled carriage with the hood up. I agreed a price but paid far too much. As advised in "Life of Brian" I should have haggled, it's expected. It was not air-conditioned but with the hood up we were out of the sun.

On the way home we had a short stop in the market, "the old bazaar in Cairo," and back at the hotel the taxi driver tried to overcharge us of course, but we stuck rigidly to our original agreed price. The next day was spent in the Egyptian Museum, which was overwhelming, crammed with exhibits but with insufficient information in English. We went from there back to the bazaar for a more thorough exploration and search for bargains. It was somewhere in this labyrinth that my badminton playing steward friend once found a valuable cache of vintage Dinky toys, new in their original boxes.

Tel Aviv in Israel was one our routes too, but they had agreed not to mark our passports, as it was rumoured that if they had then the Arabs may not have let us in. I took the opportunity on a rare four-day trip to go on a tour with other crew members around some of the sights. On this tour we visited Nazareth, the river Jordan and the Sea of Galilee where we stopped for a fish supper. The fish was tilapia, introduced under its tourist board name of "St Peter's fish." On the way back we stopped at the Israelis' favourite tourist spots, a kibbutz and a display of wrecked Arab tanks.

On our other free day on this trip we had time for a wander around the local market area, where three of the stewardesses were looking for bargains in jewellery. They started with the spiel about being British Airways crew and would that get them discounts. And of course they were offered excellent discounts as a result. After over an hour of this they tried a change of tack. They just looked at the goods and waited, and the stall-holder made the first move by offering excellent discounts. One of the girls asked just why they were being offered these discounts and was told candidly, "Just to make it interesting!"

I was an active member of the Aldershot model aircraft club at the time, and found the opportunity to take five friends from the club to the training centre for a ride in the Tristar simulator. This was before privatisation, when money was not so tight and before Security procedures put all forms of fun out of reach. Each of the modellers took a turn of flying in the Captain's seat, while I occupied my usual seat on the right. They all found the aircraft much harder to fly than they had expected. Even the chap who had a private pilot's licence would not have been able to make a safe landing on the runway without help. Then we tried another scenario, in which both pilots had taken ill during flight and four hundred holidaymakers and cabin crew were at the mercy of two model flyers in the pilot's seats.

Having a flight engineer as well was their stroke of luck as on their own they had no idea how to use the radio to contact a knowledgeable and helpful pilot/controller, played by me. I was able to talk them through programming the autopilot (still engaged fortuitously) for a fully automatic and safe landing. The guys were really delighted with their experience, especially the safe autoland.

My turn to work Christmas, away from my family, came with a trip to Port of Spain on Trinidad in the Caribbean. I never had to be away for Christmas on Trident so I suppose I was overdue for one. The crew all had a good time, helped by the rum punch and food laid on by the hotel, but there was always a twinge of loneliness. And I was still busy with my first book. Sometimes crew could take family members on Christmas trips but this one had the complication that the flight engineer and I had to fly as passengers to Antigua, spend a couple of days and then operate home, arriving on Hogmanay (New Year's Eve, but in the morning). Taking family would be too complicated. I did develop a taste for Pina Colada at the beach bar in Antigua, however.

Yes, trips to the Caribbean were available to us junior pilots, but in the winter. In spring and summer they were monopolised by senior people. The same went for North America, while my trips to the lucrative middle east usually coincided with Ramadan. Life was still interesting. Bermuda, even in winter, was very pleasant and we sampled the local cocktail, the "Dark and Stormy" made with dark rum and ginger beer, and had lively crew parties.

The beaches were lined with signs warning about the dangers of the Portuguese man-o'war, a jellyfish with very long venomous tentacles and a characteristic air-sack on the surface. Put me off swimming for good, that did. My good friend John was stung there, I heard later, and found it extremely unpleasant. From Port of Spain many crew took a trip on days off to nearby Tobago, said to be better than Trinidad, but I had a book to write.

I had one trip that ended late evening in Philadelphia, with time off next day, and this was summer—July fourth no less. I remembered a quote from W.C. Fields, "I went to Philadelphia once, but it was closed." I had the same problem. Even the diners, sandwich shops and Chinese restaurants were closed for Independence Day. I had several trips to Baltimore which was much better. I forget the hotel, but remember the crew heading for a big modern shopping mall overlooking the harbour where we habitually enjoyed an American breakfast.

And one morning a grey ship arrived and docked right below where we sat, flying the UK flag. After breakfast we wandered down and spoke to the crew on duty at the gangplank. Since berthing formalities were complete, and we had several pretty girls in our group, we were invited on board to the NCOs' mess, and shown around the ship, H.M.S. Portsmouth, including the spot where an Argentinian bomb had struck but failed to explode. None of the Falklands crew were still on board, so we heard no personal stories.

Montreal in winter was a junior trip, and I had several. The temperature was well below freezing, but you could get about using underground walkways that linked most of the hotels, shops and restaurants in the city centre. The best trip though was a long one with three or four days off and seven of us went skiing. I had never skied, but went prepared with thermal underwear, anoraks, salopettes and gloves. I found that on trips like this there is always someone who knows things, and sure enough we were led to the bus to Mont Saint-Sauveur, a ski resort 45 minutes north of Montreal in the Laurentian Mountains. We had perfect blue skies, perfect white snow, and temperatures of minus 20 Celsius. We organised a big chalet to stay overnight, and I looked for a ski school.

Now, I can speak French, I learned it at school, and French people seem to understand me, but when they reply they do so in French and it goes right over my head. They speak too fast (or I listen too slowly). The instructor that first day spoke rapid-fire French and I learned nothing. I spent most of the day on my back watching four-year-old Canadians whizz past on either side. The following day I paid for a private lesson with an English speaker and made enough progress to want more.

I normally avoided the two-week Mauritius trip because it would keep me away from the family for so long, but eventually I saw one that I could get during school holidays. It took a great deal of arranging. I had to check that the Captain would release crew seats if necessary, and didn't have the same idea himself. Because the family passed through Khartoum they needed Sudanese visas, just in case, and several vaccinations. I had to get the staff tickets, arrange the extra hotel room, and generally plan a family holiday in the tropics. I would leave first on the Sunday and get as far as Khartoum.

Then I would wait there for the Tuesday flight with my family on board to arrive Wednesday morning and fly them to Mauritius for a week on the beach. We were all excitedly looking forward to it, but when the Sunday of my departure came, so did news of a military coup toppling the Sudanese Government and closing the country. My flight went as far as Cairo, and came back. We were all bitterly disappointed at missing our holiday, but some unfortunate crew was stuck in strife-torn Khartoum for weeks, poor souls. The joys of the Jetset!

Sometimes trips came in handy. On one Athens nightstop in wet wintry weather I changed in the hotel and rushed down to jump into a taxi. I gave the driver a list of hotel addresses and we drove around them. After an hour I picked one and booked it for a family holiday in the late spring. We did not want to get caught out again in a place so near the flightpath that we could not sleep. The one I picked turned out so good that we returned for more, and my parents used it too.

There was a flight from Heathrow to Paris every hour on the hour. The double Paris was one of my regular trips. We would fly the one-hour trip to Charles de Gaulle, spend one hour on the ground, one hour back to Heathrow, an hour on the ground, one hour back to Paris, an hour on the ground, another hour back to Heathrow and finish. That's an eight-and-a-half-hour day including four flying hours, the pre-flight briefing and post flight procedure. On one such a trip the ground engineer entered the cockpit nearing the end of the first hour on the Paris parking apron, "Capt, I fink we got a problem!" He was not French.

"The rear cargo door is stuck open so I've come for the 'andle to wind it shut. Shouldn't take long."

The door to the small rear cargo bay had an electric motor whose drive shaft went into a gearbox with two output shafts, one to each side of the door. Just in case the electric power was off or the motor failed, a manual winding handle had been placed in the cockpit. The ground engineer took the handle to engage in the gearbox and wind the door shut. Dick Cross the flight engineer in our crew went with him for moral support and professional interest. My involvement in aeroplanes started after the engineer signed the Tech Log confirming it was good to go, so I continued reading my model aeroplane magazine, all our checks having been completed as far as possible. After quite a while the two engineers returned to report to the Captain, "No good, the motor must be seized, won't turn at all. I'll get me tools and the manuals."

The Captain was forced to apologise to the passengers for the delay, but unable to forecast when we might depart. The ground staff started working on plans B and C. Time passed with no favourable word from the workers below, and plan B was put into action. Our passengers disembarked to fill seats in other Heathrow-bound aircraft. From time-to-time Dick wandered down onto the tarmac to watch the ground engineers, and report back to the pilots.

"He is trying to remove the seized motor, but it is jammed," then an hour later, "The motor is off but the manual handle still will not turn the gearbox," another hour and, "It must be the gearbox that is seized so they are trying to disconnect it from the door mechanism." The ground staff's plan C, a chartered flight to carry all the remaining passengers, departed.

I went down with Dick to have a look at the work, from a respectful distance. I could see that the motor was gone, and that the steel gearbox output shafts were connected to the door mechanism by short lengths of plain steel tube. I leaned over to Dick and whispered, "If it were me I'd have taken a hacksaw to those two connecting tubes, drop the door manually and lock it shut then, as the first shepherd said to the second shepherd, we can get the flock out of here." Dick stared back as if I had insulted his entire profession.

"You can't just cut it up, you have to do it properly and follow the manuals!" I hastily retreated before I annoyed any more professional engineers, and went back to my magazine. Twenty minutes later both engineers returned to the cockpit, beaming. The Paris engineer in charge told the Captain, "You'll be on your way in five minutes."

That was the cue for me to contact ATC to arrange departure clearance in ten minutes (engineers use longer minutes than we do). But I overheard him saying, "What we done, we 'acksawed through the connecting tubes, lowered the door and my chaps are locking it from inside while I write up the book and sign it off."

In 1985 some lucrative routes to Saudi Arabia were taken from BA and handed to British Caledonian, in exchange for a couple of their loss-making routes to Rio and Sao Paulo in Brazil. It was a form of government subsidy to an ailing BCal. I seldom went to Saudi on Bidline anyway, so I didn't care much, though it niggled that the government was favouring one group of shareholders over the general public, and me. However, good did come of it. I landed a Rio trip.

I thought Rio de Janeiro would be a nice change. Some of the senior guys scoffed, "You want to fly all that way, hours and hours, and get mugged on the street when you get there?"

But I had never been to Brazil and was excited to give it a go. As it turned out the flight down there was not too bad. Because of the flight time limitations, it had been agreed that extra crew were needed. Crew control had to find an additional co-pilot to give the Captain and co-pilot some rest time in the bunk, and an additional flight engineer. I was the extra (or heavy) co-pilot who was present for take-off and landing but not at the controls. I had to have some bunk time too, just in case I was needed later, so I was sent first, and managed to get a bit of sleep.

Then I sat first in the co-pilot's seat while he went off to the bunk, then when he returned I sat in the Captain's seat until an hour before landing when the Captain returned refreshed and ready to brief the whole crew for his landing. Our hotel was right on the steeply shelving shore at the end of Leblon beach, with access from the road into reception which turned out to be on about level 8, I took the lift (elevator) to my room down about level 5, while level 1 was the beach.

We had a great time in Rio, lasting many days. We were paid our living allowances in advance, in US dollars, and advised to change it into the local currency a little at a time as the exchange rate varied daily—it went from something like 7000 to 8000 cruzeiros (Cr$) to the U.S. dollar in a week. That's serious inflation! Notes started at Cr$1000 and went up to 50000 or 100000. We were also advised to carry our money tucked inside a sock, and nothing but 10

USD in our pocket to hand over if we were ever threatened. As it turned out, nobody in the crew was ever mugged, we all had a great time and found the Brazilians friendly and welcoming, especially the women.

The days were spent sightseeing in Rio, walking along the fantastic sandy beaches and watching the fit tanned people playing volleyball, jogging, or just soaking up the sunshine. We walked the length of Leblon beach, on to Ipanema, and took a taxi along the coast to Copacabana. I met up with a couple of the stewards and we took a taxi to the Corcovado, the 700-metre-high peak overlooking the city, on which stands "Christ the Redeemer" a 30m high statue on a pedestal another 8m high. The impressive statue of Christ faces Sugar loaf mountain and overlooks the city and its setting is spectacular.

Another taxi ride took us to Sugar Loaf Mountain, or rather the hill near it, from which a two-stage cable car ride took us to the top of Sugar Loaf, looking down from which we could see the city spread out below, including Rio's secondary airport Santos Dumont. We were looking right down the runway, just off the centreline, and could see the approach slope guidance lights showing us high, above the slope. Aircraft approaching the runway would have to be below us, and as we looked down we could see them coming in from the seaward side and turning onto finals between us and the airport.

The days were spent sightseeing, but the nights, oh those Rio nights! We had arrived in the morning and crashed for a few hours' sleep, but on the first evening one of the stewardesses cornered the flight deck crew and asked if we would accompany her to this nightclub she had heard about, from somewhere (her father was a Captain). It was a seedy establishment in a dubious neighbourhood, thus the demand for four or five males for company.

We all sat at small tables, backs to the wall facing a raised platform. Some waitresses dressed as night-fighters took our drinks orders, and later the floor-show appeared on stage, a young athletic couple who were very intimate on stage in a number of interesting and unusual positions. When they left, the nightfighters returned and started trying to pick off any isolated pilot too far from the group (I'm talking inches here). I was right up against Fiona trying to look like a couple. She didn't mind as that's what her male escorts were there for, and we were left alone. One of the team, an engineer I think, was pinned to his seat at one point by a pair of thighs until he ordered drinks.

On the second evening I went with the crew to a pub called the "Lord Jim," apparently a well-known place where English was understood, for a meal, a drink, and a chat with the other crew members and anyone who spoke English in fact. Our command of Portuguese could not be relied upon, other than to order a beer. From there I went along with two stewards and three girls to a night club for more drinking and dancing and a taxi back to the hotel.

The next evening the whole crew went out for an excellent dinner in a restaurant at the horse racing track, and occupied a large table with a great view of the track and a short stroll from the bookies, where a few of the crew placed bets. One tall stewardess called Sarah won money, and rushed off after the race to collect her winnings. She came back with a fistful of cash and huge smile on her face. That made her evening, though later she confessed to having bet Cr$10,000 (about £1) on each horse in the race to be sure of winning. At least she recovered her stake money.

Sarah did not come with us the following night as she was vegetarian, and we went to a charuscurria, then a unique Brazilian speciality, but available all over the world these days. For meat eaters it was heaven. Meat waiters came to the table with carving knives and a skewer, on which was speared one of a great variety of meats, including pork, lamb, chicken, duck, ham, and of course mainly beef in a variety of cuts. The meats were cooked on the skewers, which were all clustered around a big charcoal fire. A waiter would pick up a skewer, bring it to the table, tell us what meat and what cut he had brought, and carve off a helping to anyone who wanted some.

There was also a buffet table with a selection of potato dishes, rice, vegetables and salads. Rather than pester the guests, each person has a plastic or cardboard disc, which you leave green side up if you are open to offers of additional food, or red side up if you have enough on your plate.

On my last but one evening in Rio we booked dinner and a cultural show at a place called Plataforma, which was amazing. The dinner was excellent and the show was like a mini carnival, featuring rhythmic and pervasive samba music, but this was indoors, and on a stage that thrust right out into the audience. There were musicians and dancers in glamorous costumes that ranged from just tassels and string, to giant metal and fabric constructions that swooped around the stage like graceful Daleks but featured the face of the beautiful woman inside to confirm the human connection. The whole of the crew with whom I arrived, plus a few from another crew, made our table numbers up to 17, and the whole bill, dinner and show, came to 3.5 million cruzeiros, less than maybe £20 each.

On our last evening we were picked up from the hotel for a night flight home that included a few hours in a bunk which made it so much easier, and so much safer than an approach and landing by two dead-tired zombies. Our flight was landed by a pilot who had been in the bunks until an hour before, and as heavy crew I had been on duty for the latter two thirds of the cruise. When later I watched the movie "Blame it on Rio" with Michael Caine, the whole atmosphere of the film struck a chord and reminded me of my long trip to Rio.

Captain Brian Day (or Capt. B.Day to those who watched too many Carry On films) was a training captain, and I was just the safety pilot on the fourth seat on a trip to Bermuda, Montego Bay, Kingston (Jamaica) and back through Bermuda. He kindly gave me the short sector Kingston to Bermuda; that means I did the take-off and landing. And what a landing.

We arrived in Bermuda with quite a thump, not enough to call out the ground engineers, but hard enough to be highly embarrassing. Next time I saw Captain Day we were on a Paris flight and his opening line was "Have you given up crashing on runways yet?" but the joke was on him later as he did a similarly firm landing into Paris, whereas mine back in London was quite acceptable. It just goes to show, it can (and will) happen to anyone occasionally.

In my third year in the TriStar the decision was made to start running down the fleet since the rules governing twin engined aeroplanes flying very long flights over water (called ETOPS) had gradually been relaxed. Since 1953 twin engined airliners always had to be able to reach a suitable alternate within 60 minutes flight time when flying on one engine. So the pilots drew circles on the map whose radius approximated the distance flown on one engine in 60 minutes. The circles were centred on available airports. If your route always lay within one of the overlapping circles you were in business. As you might imagine that was impossible trans-pacific, and tricky on trans-Atlantic routes and all you needed was bad weather closing an airfield somewhere on the way and the flight was cancelled. Therefore all flights 'across the pond' used four engined aeroplanes, and later the big trijets when they appeared. However in the mid-eighties the circles for twins were extended to 90 minutes, then 120 minutes as long as the aircraft and its engines met certain redundancy and reliability criteria. The modern fanjet engines like the RB211 were now extremely reliable. Later still the circles were extended to 180 minutes, leaving very few routes that ETOPS equipped twins could not handle. The bottom line was, twins were cheaper than trijets.

So in 1986 BA decided to cut back the TriStar fleet and asked for volunteers to change to another fleet. If nobody volunteered, the most junior pilots would be dragged off kicking and screaming. Suggested alternatives were the older B747 longhaul fleet or the BAC 1-11 in shorthaul, both unattractive and Heathrow based. I was keen to move my family back to Scotland for a better quality of life. New trendy little houses near ours in Surrey, with their en-suites and utility rooms, with the same floor area as ours, went for 50% more money despite being on a smaller plot. In Scotland we could afford a really nice house that seemed always beyond our reach in Surrey, and my daughters would be near their grandparents.

Rapidly rising house prices in Surrey made a bigger house seem unaffordable, and cabin crew were often heard boasting that their house made more money than they did at work. An estate agent once told us that, "Your house is probably the most significant element of your investment portfolio." To me, it was where you lived. Then there was the neighbour who told us they were moving away to progress up the housing ladder, because money that should be invested in property was being frittered away, on luxury items "like food." I could not keep a straight face at that one. Of course they did not mean basic food, they clarified, they meant luxuries like the Saturday night Chinese take-away. The other big incentive was that friends just a little senior to me were Captains in Scotland, and I was really keen to sit in the left seat, and the twin turboprops in Scotland were my best, my only foreseeable, chance of that.

Chapter 7
Twin Turboprops

I phoned the TriStar office and asked, "Can you get me onto the HS 748 in Glasgow if I volunteer to leave TriStar?"

"Nobody ever asked that before, I'll get back to you." And so it was that a couple of months later a momentous change took place in our family life. I went on a training course in Cranebank, we house hunted hundreds of miles away, and the girls left all their friends and moved to a new school. I felt right at home back in Scotland, where nobody at work droned on about how expensive school fees were or how much their house had increased in value that week. If you want to know exactly how it felt to be home, search YouTube for "Tennents Caledonia advert" to see the video.

During my training course on the HS 748, nicknamed the "Budgie" in British Airways, the airline was sold into private hands by the government, but I hardly noticed as I was busy. However this sell-off had a profound long-term effect on the company and ultimately took the "British" out of British Airways. Over the rest of my career the company sold or gave away virtually all their operations outside London and by the time I retired had very few direct employees beyond London. And ten years after my retirement, the company's AGM for shareholders was being held in Madrid. But back to Budgies.

The course itself was old school, as was the aeroplane. The instruments were round dials, the control surfaces were manually operated, by cables and pulleys, and there was a big lever in the cockpit that locked them all so that they didn't blow around when parked in the wind. We were reminded that accidental engagement of this gust lock caused the Dan Air crash at Shetland in 1979. Overnight the controls were further locked using red painted wooden locks on the outside.

The aircraft systems were basic, with no computers at all. The digital watch that I wore had more computing power than the Budgie. It did have a rudimentary autopilot with height and heading lock that was useful in the cruise while we were busy briefing, communicating or doing paperwork. There was no simulator available, so after passing the groundschool exams we went flying in an empty aeroplane which felt wonderful as I hated simulators. I trained as a co-pilot in the right seat. We tried stalling it (no nasty deep stall), shutting down an engine to fly on one, we gravity dropped the undercarriage as if the hydraulics had failed, and all for real.

Our aircraft had either 48 or more usually 44 passenger seats, a large baggage hold right at the back and a smaller one around the front door. Passengers entered via the rear door at which a simple set of manually operated built-in airstairs was fitted. The solitary cabin crew sat at the back door and she was in charge of a tiny galley for drinks and cold snacks.

When I started in Highland Division only a hundred or so pilots in the company were junior to me. That hundred had joined in the two years after me, then none at all for eleven years. But about Budgie time, British Airways started recruiting new pilots from outside the airline. Most had been with other airlines, waiting patiently for their chance. Some of them were women, actual female pilots, a very rare species about which little was known. Their blouses buttoned the other way, I noticed, and they turned out to be very pleasant and capable, and crucially all were junior to me.

Highland Division was set up as a low-cost entity separate from Mainline British Airways with a main base in Glasgow and our own Flight Manager, operations, engineering, roster department and administration. It was a more friendly and sociable workplace than I was used to in London. The crews all got to know each other, the managers, and operations and admin staff. We had a big staff dance every Christmas, as well as smaller parties in the Clansman Club for birthdays or when somebody retired or left the base. I joined the badminton club and someone organised some trips to a local indoor go-kart track and a paint-balling venue (I missed the paint-balling unfortunately). A few of our island destinations closed on Sundays (quite right too) and there were no flights on Christmas or New Year.

One of the cost-saving measures was that staff at destinations were reduced to an absolute minimum, and the pilots helped out. We did our own engineering cover, signing off the Tech Log for the next flight, overseeing refuelling when necessary and so on. We tried to load enough fuel at Glasgow for the day, since fuel was very expensive away from the Glasgow base. We helped loading and unloading baggage and freight, and we completed our own weight and balance charts and loadsheet.

Flights were operated to Inverness and the western isles, the northern Orkney isles, and the Shetlands and Aberdeen from where the oilfields were serviced by a large helicopter fleet. We also flew from Glasgow and Edinburgh to Belfast, Manchester and Birmingham. At the time I joined we even operated flights from West Berlin to cities in West Germany, in conjunction with mainline BA.

The British Airways "German Internal" network had come about as a result of an agreement between the USA, France, the UK and USSR at the end of WW2 which allowed East Germany to force all flights to West Berlin to be operated by the three occupying powers and to route through 3 narrow corridors up to 10,000 feet high. No Germans were allowed, and even a Danish BA pilot could not operate to Berlin. Flights started after the war with war-surplus DC3 aircraft, called the Dakota (or just Dak) in BEA service, along with Pionair, Viking and Elizabethan piston-engined airliners, and later the Viscount, BAC 1-11, and in my time the Boeing 737 and HS 748. All our cabin crew were locally recruited Germans, and all girls I think.

The HS 748 twin turboprop involvement was due to a downturn in business, and the decision to axe some of the routes because the operating costs of the Boeing 737 resulted in losses, and reducing the number of flights in the day only made it worse. Somebody in management had a bright idea—change to the smallest and cheapest aeroplanes the airline owned, the low-profile HS 748 in Scotland. "Never heard of it!" was the attitude of most board members (OK I wasn't there so I made that quote up). But figures were produced that showed the turboprop could make these routes viable. It would mean promoting a few new captains and maybe acquiring a couple of extra aircraft, but hey, it was cheap so they went for it. The strange thing is that once it was making money they added additional flights per day, and that made more money so they increased the frequency again. It became so good that they wanted a bigger and better turboprop, but that comes later.

About this time British Caledonian was about to go bust, so the government decreed that the newly privatised British Airways would take them over, but for political reasons it was to be presented as a merger. The new airline after the 'merger' took the British from BCal and Airways from BA to become British

Airways. Because it was presented as a merger the ex-BCal pilot force was merged with ours resulting in many of us losing seniority, and seniority was crucial.

I shelved that first book, having too much fun to be bothered in Highland Division, and even away in Berlin I hardly touched the book. We spent four or five days at a time in Berlin, flying four flights a day with either the morning or evening off to sightsee, shop or eat. After one particular evening meal in Berlin I was up half the night with food poisoning, and next day found that the Captain with me had it too. We were surprised to have food hygiene problems in Germany, but you just never know.

Since most passengers were German I learned enough German for a cabin address, sticking to the same place and same script each time. A few of the German cabin crew girls were enthusiastic and keen to help correct my German, but most did not like the Budgie. I think they felt lonely on their own in the cabin, most preferring the team of four on the Boeing 737.

After departing Berlin Tegel we flew over East Germany at low level, 6000 to 8000 feet along the prescribed corridors. The low-level corridors meant that we flew through any bad weather, instead of over it. The East Germans watched to ensure we stuck to the route and our own radar controllers kept an eye on the Germans, and often would report what looked like a fighter near us but no pilot I spoke to had seen one. My theory was that while the USA had stealth bombers invisible to radar, the Soviets had invented stealth fighters that did show up on radar, causing alarm, but could never be seen visually, as they didn't actually exist.

On one evening in Berlin a bunch of us pilots went for a meal together. I had my usual meal of beef in pepper sauce served with gratin potatoes and some kind of coleslaw on the side, washed down with a beer. I knew most of the captains with whom I was flying but we didn't meet other co-pilots as much, so I still didn't know some of them. Although I was on the late pick-up next day, after one beer I switched to orange juice. Shortly thereafter the early crews got up to leave, to allow themselves the requisite bottle to throttle time, all except John Shaw's co-pilot whom I didn't know. He told them, "Carry on, I'll be right behind you!" then ordered another drink. I'll call him Billy.

Half an hour later Arthur, the captain with whom I was flying, moved beside Billy and told him, in a most forthright manner, "You need to leave, RIGHT NOW, get to bed and be ready for the morning!" Billy was obviously shaken, and moved off without a word. A couple of hours later we had paid and were leaving when the crews flying the late inbound flights arrived. One of them said he had seen Billy drinking alone in a bar up the street, and wondered why. Arthur was furious. He stormed into the bar and dragged Billy out. He had to as Billy couldn't stand, never mind walk. That seemed to be that, cancel his flights tomorrow and the rest of Billy's career, but Arthur had an idea.

Arthur explained that I had enough time off and had stopped drinking hours earlier, and so I was the only person who could legally fly with John next morning. He asked if I would do it. More for the sake of Highland Division than for the drunken Billy, I reluctantly agreed. Arthur agreed to take on Billy for the late flights next day, and march him in to face management on return to Glasgow.

So next morning I was down in the hotel lobby a little early for pickup, to explain things to John, but where was John? Surely he hadn't slept in? He came down right on pickup time, blazing mad. He had just come from Billy's room, having battered the door until it opened. But Billy was incoherent and unable to explain that I had taken over his flights, so John was on his way to cancel the flights. I filled him in on the swap deal if he would have me, and that Arthur would deal with Billy.

True to his word, Arthur returned to Glasgow with Billy and told him he would report fully to the manager, but gave him the opportunity to get there first to confess all and beg for help. Amazingly the company sent him to a drying out clinic and he returned to flying a few weeks later. I would not have been so sympathetic, especially when I heard that it had all happened before. The company was incredibly sympathetic to this guy but, after he fell off the wagon yet again, he was eventually fired.

After the rigid procedures of Heathrow, it felt incredibly liberating to fly around Scotland. We were in touch with Scottish radar the whole time, though there was seldom other traffic for them to report and steer us around. We could often see our destination from a very long way off in good clear weather, and would call them up and be "cleared for a visual approach, no other traffic," looking out of the windows the whole way in.

Even Glasgow and Edinburgh were flexible enough to offer visual circuit approaches which saved time and fuel and our small aircraft could use the smaller cross-runways if they offered a shorter or more into-wind approach. We always were on the lookout for shortcuts, like visual circuits, and sometimes if the weather was clear and smooth we would fly lower than usual to give the passengers wonderful views of the highlands and islands worth many times their fare.

On other days of course we coped with howling winds, giving a bumpy ride, and low cloud and poor visibility requiring all our skill to break cloud in just the right place to see the runway and make a dart for the landing spot. Getting the Budgie down and keeping it down was not the end of our troubles as after parking facing into wind we would have to open the front door and try to unload the bags, mail and freight without letting the wind blow them away across the apron and out to sea.

It was still better than the tedium of endless identical approaches to Heathrow. The Budgie had no APU to provide warm air on the ground, so for the first time I had to fly in wintertime with my jacket on, which felt restrictive. I much preferred flying in shirt sleeves.

A new batch of cabin crew started in Glasgow, the smallest of whom, Chrissie, was a lovely girl with a charming permanent smile and bubbly personality. It turned out she was under the minimum height for a BA stewardess but she had impressed the Flight Manager at interview. She kept the job too because Flight Managers don't admit to mistakes, and the truth was he really fancied her. We ALL really fancied her.

One day flying back to Glasgow with Graeme as captain it was my turn to land, but the weather was close to my limits. BA imposed cross-wind limits on co-pilots two thirds that of the Captain's limits. Graeme said, "Carry on for now but I may have to take it. The wind might get worse, then again it may drop. We'll just see how it goes."

I relished the challenge but not the uncertainty so replied, "If you would really rather land it yourself just decide now then we both know where we stand." So he did the landing, no big deal. I was due for a command course sometime soon. Then I could decide.

In Command

I had been in BA for fourteen years by the time I had a chance to become a Captain, but most of my course mates stayed in London and remained co-pilots. A couple saw the light, and opportunity, and were with me in Glasgow. I passed the command course and became the man who signed the Tech Log, in several places many times a day, and the load sheets, and my signature became as undecipherable as any doctor's. I decided to learn a little Gaelic from a book, as

I had taken the trouble to say a few words in German on Berlin flights and thought our own people deserved as much. I utterly failed to learn the language, but undaunted I wrote out a cabin address, and asked one of the staff at Stornoway to translate it into Gaelic. I still could not read it so I asked for a phonetic pronunciation and wrote that out as well, then practised saying it. Thereafter I did the welcome on board and goodbye cabin addresses in Gaelic and then English on all my flights to and from the western isles, Benbecula and Stornoway.

Once in command I could really relish the freedom. Often we would check in at Glasgow in the morning and take an aeroplane away for the day, four or six sectors without contacting management or operations. I was my own boss for the day. We built up our experience very quickly. As a new Captain in Highland I was not allowed to give away a sector to the co-pilot until I had done seventy-five landings myself, but that took only six weeks. In serious longhaul flying that could have taken four or even five years.

The US Navy's shooting down of Iran Air 655 with 290 people on board came as a shock. There had been other incidents, but this was a scheduled flight on its usual flight path in Iranian airspace over Iranian territorial waters. I had recently been on TriStar operating in the Gulf, and I was thinking that could so easily have been us. The excuse offered was that they mistook a climbing Airbus for a diving F-14 Tomcat, but nobody, as far as I know, was ever disciplined over such a catastrophic blunder. When passing over a grey Navy ship off Skye I remember the jokes: "I hope that's not the Iranian Navy."

"As long as it's not the US Navy we'll be fine."

A few months after I became a Captain, BA management took on a modern enlightened image, they "saw the light" or perhaps they were shown it by a PR company with great powers of persuasion and a great gift for making money out of thin air. This manifested itself to me in a letter from management giving details of a two-day residential course that would appear on my roster with few other details besides a crew ticket to Heathrow, a coach to the venue, and dress was to be smart but informal.

The coach took us to a classy country hotel, and after checking in and leaving my luggage in my room I headed for the conference room to meet the other participants, many of whom had made their own way directly by car. The course was composed entirely of Captains, of whom I was the newest and youngest. The introductory talk by the human relations guru emphasised how important it was for aircrew to get along together as a team, that the Captain was the focal point of the team, and this had all come about because of the intake of new co-pilots, which had started the year before as a trickle but was becoming a flood. I looked around the room. Many of those present were crusty old Captains or senior co-pilots when I joined, and had not seen a new entry pilot for fifteen years. In contrast I had already met the first intake, including a couple of the women, and had flown with them.

After a pleasant lunch break we were broken into groups for discussions on the implications of flying with new pilots, but instead we discussed the capriciousness of management and where they and the government were taking our airline. Later a psychology expert asked us to consider things from the point of view of a recent recruit, who had just changed jobs, moved house, taken on a challenging training course, and then got stuck with one of us.

Dinner, with wine, was provided and the bar was free, for a couple of drinks at least. That was probably to deter the locally based chaps from driving home, and staying there. The rooms were very comfortable, breakfast was generous and well cooked, and then boredom resumed in the conference room. Shortly after lunch a coach took us back to Heathrow. My overall impressions of the course were that all the information I had gathered in two days could have been written on one side of a sheet of A4 paper and handed out to each Captain at check-in, and that the con-men who ran the courses were highly skilled in extracting money from their marks.

What a waste! Further extravagant courses, involving a much wider range of senior employees than just Captains, followed in later years, including 'Putting People First,' and 'Putting People First 2, the sequel.' My abiding impressions of those events were the waste of money, management ineptitude (but a B plus for at least trying), good food, and how to remember somebody's name. We were told to picture the person in a guise or activity suggested by their name, like Cooper building a barrel, or Brooke jumping a stream.

Every pilot, on each night in Berlin, donated a couple of Deutschmarks from his allowances to a fund. This fund was used to provide leisure activities and club memberships in West Berlin, and also to pay for a lavish annual party to which were invited all the pilots and cabin crew who were in Berlin that evening but not on duty, plus the ground staff and other airport workers and local VIPs. The date of the party was always announced after the rosters were published so it was just your lucky day if you could go. I went to the party my first year as a Captain, and had a good time.

A beautiful stewardess called Petra seemed very friendly, danced with me a bit and stuck close. I was beginning to think I must have something after all but eventually one of my colleagues confided to me the reason. Petra was being pestered by a creepy fire truck driver or some such, and wanted to give the impression that she was in a relationship. Eventually the fireman cleared off and later as the party fizzled out Petra went home alone. At least for much of the evening I had a little ego boost, and it certainly was a great party.

I heard a story that at another Berlin party, some years before, some local Berlin dignitaries had been invited, and one of them, a pompous little man, cornered a very senior captain and came round to asking him, by way of small talk, which of the many aircraft that had been used on the Berlin run had been the most effective, and the captain told him "The Lancaster," and walked off.

Another old favourite "Don't mention the war!" story told on such occasions was a supposed exchange with a ground controller who, when being asked to give more explicit taxying instructions, said peevishly, "Have you not been to Frankfurt before?" to which the senior captain replied, "Yes, twice, but it was dark, and we didn't land."

Later that same year, just before Christmas, came the news that a PanAm B747 crashed into Lockerbie taking out a row of houses, killing everyone on board and many Lockerbie residents. It was a tragic blow to everyone in the aviation industry, and we were reminded of it as we passed by on every cross-border flight to Manchester and Birmingham. I changed my cabin address after that, avoiding mentioning Lockerbie and referring instead to passing Dumfries rather than allude to the terrorist threat we all faced.

I already said that the Glasgow base was friendly, and it did not take long to get on first name terms with all the staff in the Scottish network, and even the Tower in Stornoway as we often visited Gordon and his team during the long midweek turnarounds. Some days we had three or four hours to spend in Stornoway, and we could pass the time talking to Gordon and the local BA staff during their quiet times. Or we could borrow the company car and drive into town for lunch in one of several good hotels.

Sometimes we went further afield to visit the ancient (pre-pyramids) standing stone circle at Callanish, or the ruins (pre-Roman) of the Broch at

Carloway, or just stroll along a deserted snow-white sandy beach of which there are several on Lewis and Harris.

Now that I was the captain, all the instant go/stop, land/go-around decisions were mine. On one occasion the weather at Kirkwall in the Orkneys was legal though doubtful, but to look on the bright side we might find a gap in the cloud and land, so I decided to set off. The only landing aid was a VOR/DME, which is the beacon that transmits a coded signal along the approach track lined up with the runway, along with a distance away. I briefed the co-pilot to fly along the runway track and descend 300 feet per mile to a point a mile from the runway. If I see the runway from there I say "Land" and take control. If not, he flies a go-around.

We were still in cloud and I saw nothing when he called "Decide," so I called "Go-around!" but during his go-around I saw the runway through breaks in the cloud, so we had another go hoping the breaks in the cloud would be just where we needed them this time. No luck second time, or third time (so much for third time lucky!). Back we went to Aberdeen with our disappointed (but alive) passengers. Next day we did exactly the same, and again we came tantalisingly close, but without better radio aids we had done our best. If only the government had spent the money for an ILS system!

The ILS is a much more accurate radio landing aid that gives precise position information in three dimensions. The Trident and TriStar could use Cat 3 ILS to land on unseen runways in thick fog, but the Budgie's Cat 1 equipment was far less sophisticated and we had to see the runway from about half a mile and 200 feet to have a chance of landing. Aberdeen initially had only one Cat 1 ILS, but a few years later following an over-run accident after a downwind landing, a second was installed at the other end. However the one at Stornoway was removed, which often left us groping around there in low cloud hoping for a glimpse of the runway, like at all the other Highlands and Islands airports. Having an ILS had made Stornoway seem like a proper airport.

Maybe that's why Pan Am dropped in once. It was a wide body twin (Airbus A310 I think) on a trans-Atlantic ETOPS flight westbound. Some while after passing over the Stornoway beacon, their last landfall before the Atlantic tracks, a fault required the shutting down of one of the engines, and the last line of the shutdown drill on a twin reads "Land at the nearest suitable airfield." Their fancy electronic map screen would show Stornoway airport so they would have looked it up.

The runway was short (for them) but adequate, there was an ILS (must be a proper airport then) and British Airways operated several flights a day, and had a company frequency, another bonus point, as ground handling would be available. Decision made, they informed Scottish ATC, called Gordon in the Tower ("A what? Iain, check our runway can take the weight") and the BA office, and in they came for a perfect landing on one engine. Then what? The taxiways were too narrow for a wide body aircraft, so they left tyre ruts in the grass at the corners, but made it to the apron. Big aircraft don't have airstairs built in, and Stornoway's backup set of rusty steps didn't reach halfway to an A310's door so they improvised. A tall forklift truck with something like a wooden garden shed bolted on to the fork was hoisted to the door, loaded with the first dozen passengers and lowered to the ground. Then up again for the next dozen, and so on. It took a while, but was better than damaging ankles using emergency slides.

Pan Am sent a couple of narrow body jets (with airstairs) from Germany to pick up the passengers, and a spare engine with engineers. They didn't have the proper lifting gear and had to make do (that forklift again?) but the job was done and all the aircraft had left, leaving only the tyre tracks in the grass, by the time I next flew in to hear all about it from Alec, D.R. and Donnie, our ground staff.

After the Air India bomb in 1985 and Lockerbie in 1988 security was tightened up all over. The formal procedures were not rigorously applied on the islands but security, however informal, was watertight, as everybody knew everybody and would have been aware of anyone acting suspiciously. For the same reason there was very little crime on the islands. When we took the company car for lunch or sightseeing we didn't lock it. I felt guilty of lack of trust just taking out the key. The BA manager in Benbecula, Martin, said that the key in his motor bike was rusted in permanently, as he had never removed it.

I remember one small child visiting the cockpit after a flight and standing silent once he realised I did not understand him. His father said the boy spoke only Gaelic as he had not yet started school, but that was unusual. Among people of my own generation and older in the Highlands and Islands, it was more common for children to learn English as a foreign language at primary school. Thus they learned to speak properly and without a strong local accent like Cockneys, Scousers, Geordies or Glaswegians.

The Northern isles, the Orkneys and Shetlands, were never Gaelic speaking. They have been part of Scotland for many, many centuries, regained from the

Vikings after battles, peace negotiations or as marriage dowries, but they never lost their Norse heritage. Sumburgh airport has two runways, runway 09/27 runs east/west across an isthmus (like Gibraltar) and is much shorter than Gib. Runway 15/33 is a good length for Budgies, but there is high ground at both ends and no radio aids to speak of.

The first time I went there, as extra crew just to see it, I was amazed to be looking UP at the lighthouse as we passed close by. On the approach to 33 we had to break cloud well to the south so that we could see the Gibraltar-like tower of rock on which is perched the lighthouse. As we came closer our aiming point became the quarry on the hillside below, and when we were very near the quarry we dipped the left wingtip into a farmyard, which wheeled us round to line up nicely with the runway. Nothing to it, but you dare not lose sight of that rock.

Sumburgh airport was a busy place, with helicopter traffic to and from the many oil rigs in the northern sector of the North Sea. There was a demand for early flights out in the morning so we had a crew stay overnight. In Highland Division fashion, we lifted the car keys from the hook in the office, threw our bags in the car and drove ourselves to the 'hotel.' An accommodation block had been built by the oil industry, with comfortable rooms, a restaurant and of course a large bar where the all-male oil workers drank, played games and drank.

The BA crew occupied three rooms each night, and we were welcomed in and allowed to use the pool table, a disaster of a game for me. One night there, our stewardess Anne overwhelmed both of us pilots, and then proceeded to beat every oil worker who challenged her. I also remember a summer party in Shetland, and a walk along the beach, with the water gently lapping on the sand, and still with enough light left in the sky at midnight to read a newspaper.

Another time we were heading into Shetland, who told us when we called that a southerly wind was blowing a bank of fog in towards the airfield, so we better be quick. It was to be a race, so we put the nose down to dive on some speed and hurried straight towards the airfield. As we came near we could see the fog bank, and it was going to be a close-run thing. If the fog covered the runway before we could land we would have to go all the way back to Aberdeen, so we flew low on a tight downwind leg past the runway, and then a tight right turn took us onto final approach to runway 15.

When on short finals we could see the far end of the runway disappear in the fog, crossing the hedge we could still see the middle so we landed, and as we turned off the runway the fog enveloped us and we had to grope our way to the familiar allotted parking spot.

The flying on Highland Division was occasionally inspiring, as on one beautiful day when flying from Stornoway to Glasgow we elected to fly lower than usual to take advantage of the beautiful views as we swept in over Loch Torridon from the Minch, and after passing Diabaig and Inveralligin we crossed Loch Torridon. Our route followed a valley towards Stromeferry at the narrows of Loch Carron, and as we did so we climbed to clear the highland mountains ahead. The views of the mountains were stunning, and finally we could see down the full length of Loch Lomond to Balloch and the Clyde, with the ancient volcanic plug of Dumbarton Rock visible in the distance.

Glasgow airport was quiet and allowed us a visual approach right down Loch Lomond, along the left bank of the river Leven to the Clyde, then we followed the north bank of the Clyde, flew past the Erskine bridge and turned right onto finals for runway 23 at Glasgow. Some days, it's a shame to take the money.

We flew a regular freight charter at night to Dublin carrying five tons of wastepaper (the Sun, freshly printed in Glasgow). We wasted no time. As soon as the aircraft was loaded the doors closed and we were off, climbing and calling Scottish ATC for a routing straight to Dublin, normally granted under radar control. The moment we stopped and opened the door, a loader gang started unstrapping the cargo and throwing it off onto a truck, and the moment they finished we closed up, started and set off in a straight line for Glasgow. We used to cut more than half an hour off the scheduled time as we had nobody to wait for. That was our only night flight.

The Belfast route could also be shortened by flying direct, off the Airways. One such return flight to Glasgow, on a beautiful day, passed near my model flying club's site where a friend's yellow model aeroplane had been lost in a forest two weeks earlier, and could not be found. I asked Glasgow ATC if we could position visually for runway 23, in use at the time, and they obliged. I handed control to my co-pilot Dave and asked him to "descend to circuit height and fly over that wooded area."

That would position us on the start of the downwind leg of the visual approach. It also meant I could look for the lost model, and as we flew over the woods I spotted a tiny yellow cross lying in a small clearing in the woods. I sketched the position, and then ATC were even more helpful by offering to let us land on 05, the nearer end of the runway, saving several miles. It was a quiet time and there was very little wind. I accepted the offer, took back control, dropped the wheels and flaps and landed. A few days later I dragged the rain-soaked model out through the thick undergrowth, doing more damage than the crash had done.

In my time on turboprops I had only one engine failure, and we were hardly moving on the runway at the time. Just after I opened the throttles for take-off at Glasgow doing maybe 20 knots, my co-pilot John McBoyle called "STOP." We stopped abruptly. The right engine temperature had just gone off the clock, and was still off. I ordered it shut down, and told ATC. We sat there with just the left engine running, and I said, "At least there is no fire. Maybe we could taxi back; could just be a gauge fault." Then the fire bell went off on the right engine and we fired the bottles.

"Shut down the left one too!" before I called ATC for the fire engines to come out. I told the stewardess to drop the stairs but not evacuate the passengers, not yet. Then I told John to open his side window and stick his head out, to examine the right engine for signs of fire, especially any flicker of flame, but it just looked damp with the extinguishant dribbling out of every orifice of the cowling. The fireman in the truck came on the radio and confirmed no sign of fire. I called the operations office on the second radio to send a bus for the passengers and a tow truck for the aeroplane and promised ATC we'd get out of the way asap.

The stewardess and passengers collected their belongings and walked calmly down the steps to the bus, we pulled up the steps, and were towed to the hangar where engineers looked forlornly up the tailpipe and pointed out blobs of recently-molten metal. "It's not just the gauge then!" was the verdict. It turned out to have been a failure of the propeller control which had made it turn to coarse pitch, preventing its rapid acceleration, so the turbine temperature ran away. I kept a blob of melted turbine as a souvenir.

The challenges of Highland Division varied day by day, with various combinations of extreme winds, low cloud, bad visibility, snow and ice, limited radio aids, limiting cross-winds, and very occasionally, an obnoxious passenger. Most of our passengers were delightful, even when we were an hour or two late. Their alternative, the MacBraynes ferry, could be a day or two late in bad weather. But one day at Inverness, the BA local Manager came to the cockpit to say one particular passenger had refused to be searched. He just strutted past security and boarded.

He was a "Do you know who I am?" type, the Sheriff of somewhere near Inverness. I went back to the cabin and explained to him that the aeroplane did not fly until everyone on board had satisfied the security staff, and he reluctantly went off threatening, "I'll write to Lord King, I'll complain to Colin Marshall etc," while I told the stewardess to search the coat he left behind in case it was a subtle ploy or a test of our security. He returned having been cleared by security, and we set off. The Stornoway staff at destination said he had been difficult before, and was maybe just terrified of flying and taking it out on those around. We never met again fortunately.

One wintry day in Glasgow, the whole network was thrown into chaos. There were snow showers all over, a broken-down aeroplane on some remote island airport, the wind was howling over the parked aircraft at Glasgow, rocking them around uncomfortably. It was going to be ten times worse in the air. Rostered duties were out of the window. There were five crews in the crew room waiting to see what rescue plan Operations would come up with to get as many people as possible to their destinations. The Ops man came in, and read from his prepared list. One by one the challenges awarded to each crew were detailed, and they seemed worse each time. Lastly he came to my crew. "Alasdair, you can go home. Goodnight!" It's good to be good, but it's better to be lucky.

Another lucky day, I flew to Inverness for a nightstop with co-pilot John and stewardess Veronica, who announced possession of three tickets to a concert that night in Inverness by the hugely popular Scottish rock band, Runrig. I had an album or two of theirs but had never seen them live. We hired a taxi to the venue that bleak December night, and queued outside for a while, shivering. Once inside, the concert took a while to get going but once they took the stage Runrig were amazing, ten times better live than on vinyl. It was my first live concert since I was a student and I was overwhelmed, a fan for life, and I have attended many of their concerts since.

At the end of the concert it was snowing, and all three of us tried different ploys to call a taxi. Before the days of mobile phones, it was hopeless, a hundred people waiting for two public phones. In walked the taxi driver who had taken us there and he picked out Veronica, "Will you be wanting a taxi?"

Staff travel gradually got better. I took my family with me on a four-day trip to Berlin. I flew the aeroplane by way of Manchester and Munster, we stayed in the Intercontinental Hotel, having booked an extra room for my daughters. We had a lovely time in cold but bright weather. My wife had been there on a school trip and enjoyed the nostalgia, and my daughters enjoyed the novelty. When I was away on flights they did their own thing, mainly shopping along the Ku'damm, and later we met up for dinner. We all flew home together as passengers. That year we had family holidays in Cyprus (a favourite) and Florida.

I had very little contact with management, but they could be useful. My daughters' school held a parents' dance before Christmas and parents were invited to donate prizes for the raffle, so I asked my manager, how about donating two free return tickets Glasgow to Paris, great publicity. He mulled it over and came back with two conditions. It had to rate as the first prize, and I was not allowed to win it. Done deal. At the dance I quite by chance won second prize, the only time I ever won in a raffle. We won dinner and a night in a country hotel near Edinburgh.

We were on long final for Inverness when the pilot landing ahead of us damaged his nosewheel and blocked the runway. Tower said, "We will tow it off the runway, give us twenty minutes." So we changed back to Scottish, told them the problem and outlined my plan to take the passengers sightseeing. They had no traffic to affect us so we stayed fairly low and flew slowly down Loch Ness, past Urquhart Castle and turned around and flew back. Inverness wanted another fifteen minutes, but sounded confident this time when I threatened to go to Kinloss instead. So back with Scottish I took the passengers on a tour over Inverness, Dingwall and the Black Isle and returned to see the broken aeroplane about to clear the runway so that we could eventually land.

I was flying with Claire, one of the new female co pilots (she's now a 747 Captain), and during the turnaround in Stornoway en route for a nightstop in Inverness we wandered into the cabin to say hello to the stewardess sitting down the back with her newspaper. She was evidently searching for the horoscope page, at which I scoffed, "You don't believe in that rubbish do you?" but evidently she was really into it and asked our star signs.

I wanted no part, but Claire humoured her and was read out the bland nonsense that could be taken any number of ways. Then Claire asked the stewardess to read her own, which she did. I could not have made it more explicit had I written it myself. Couched in the usual horoscope language it said she would have an intimate romantic involvement with a work colleague that night. "Oh, that means you have to sleep with me in Inverness tonight, great, looking forward to it!" Claire agreed there was no other possible interpretation, and though the stewardess's belief in horoscopes was shaken to the core, nothing else came of it.

Claire and I had another memorable flight together, late afternoon in an empty aircraft from Glasgow to Stornoway. As we set off on the usual route over Loch Lomond, it was a lovely calm day in early Spring, and the scenery was beautiful. We asked Scottish for a low level and enjoyed the view. I checked that there was no traffic around, descended some more and altered course to fly over the ski resort at Aonach Mor near Fort William. We could see individual skiers as we passed close by, then we turned west along Loch Eil, past the tall monument at Glenfinnan and the huge railway viaduct (yes the one in the Harry Potter movie) to Arisaig and on to Rhum. Turning north then took us straight up the length of Skye (with an orbit around the Cuillin mountains thrown in) and on to Stornoway.

And that reminds me of another time I was in Stornoway with Claire. We arrived late, en route to another Inverness nightstop. The wind was from 070 (just north of east) at 35 knots. No problem, that is lined up nicely with the short runway, 07, where we landed without a hitch. Passengers disembarked, others embarked and we were ready. One slight problem, the manual does not give any data for taking off on runway 07, only landing. I called Gordon in the tower to ask the wind. "Still from 070 but now 40 knots."

"I'll need to phone London from the office for take-off figures for runway 07, which could take half an hour to an hour, Gordon," and he replied, "We are supposed to close in ten minutes, can you be quick?" Our cross-wind limit was 35 knots, so it's just over the limit. Claire and I talked.

"Gordon, our limit is 35 knots cross-wind on runway 36, but we'd like to start up and taxi out and wait for a lull in the wind." So we taxied out and stopped, lined up pointing north on runway 36, waiting. After a few minutes Tower called, "The wind is reading 070 at 35, cleared for take-off." With a limiting crosswind from the right I held full right aileron, opened the throttles and we were off, straight down the centre, gradually reducing aileron, then up and away. No problem at all. "Bye, Gordon!" and changed to Scottish ATC.

End of 748, onto ATP

BA wanted a bigger and more modern turboprop for the Berlin services, with the benefit also spilling into Highland Division. They wanted an aircraft with more seats, an attractive comfortable cabin, a proper toilet, and better fuel efficiency. The British Aerospace ATP (Advanced Turbo Prop) fitted the bill and was introduced gradually, starting with Berlin services then Glasgow to Manchester and eventually the Island services. I waited until then before transferring as I preferred the Highland services to Berlin. I flew my last Berlin tour in March of 1989 as the ATP took over, but I held back from flying the ATP until January 1991. By that time the wall was down, Berlin was one big western city and the Russians were gone.

I will not say much about the ATP as few of you have seen one and they have disappeared from the scene, but they were my first aircraft with a "glass cockpit." That means that the traditional round instrument dials had been replaced by square coloured screens, like flat computer screens. The computerised glass cockpits and autopilots on all modern airliners can be programmed, to a variable extent, and gave rise to the familiar phrase on the cockpit voice recorder, "What's it doing now?"

The ATP had a few teething problems, and ATP came to stand for Another Technical Problem, but most had been resolved by the time I joined the fleet, yet another lucky decision. It certainly was more modern than the Budgie, with big, quiet, slow-turning six-bladed props running on a free turbine. The toilet was modern, like any other aeroplane toilet, the cabin had covered overhead racks and the passengers must have considered it a big improvement, until it broke down. In some respects the ATP was not as rugged as the old HS 748.

One of my colleagues was in Shetland two days before Christmas on one of those typical Shetland days when you have to tie small children to something solid or else they will blow away, and the same goes for mail bags and luggage being loaded on the ATP. The aircraft was parked, as always, facing into wind but was being buffeted around something wicked. But islanders are tough, and compared to the long hours of stomach churning on a ferry voyage, this flight was to be quick and easy—a quick buffet and you're away. They started up, taxied onto the runway, then with the wind on their backs taxied along to the end and turned to face the howling westerly wind. There was a recorded gust of 72 knots, about 83 mph, during their taxi along the runway, which even in Shetland terms is "a bit windy."

The checks were done while lined up with the brakes on, the gust locks were disengaged, and controls cross-checked (remember Dan Air), throttles opened and they were off. At "rotate" the nose came up, and so did the left wing but the right wing stayed down. The right wingtip was scraping along the ground, off the edge of the runway and making a curving gouge in the grass as it went, curving to the right of course. Eventually the crew managed to pick up the right wing out of the Shetland dirt but were now in a right turn, whereas a left turn after take-off was required to avoid high ground ahead.

Since left turns were a major problem they continued, indeed tightened, the right turn and succeeded in avoiding the high ground. It took half left aileron and a bit of left rudder just to fly straight, but they managed to reach the mainland, and decided to go for RAF Kinloss whose runway was closer, longer and had less crosswind than Aberdeen's. The landing was tricky but entirely successful.

Investigation showed that the extra-strong gust from behind, while taxying downwind along the runway before take-off, had damaged the operating mechanism of the right aileron. After that British Airways placed strict limits on the amount of wind we were allowed for ground operations (taxying) covering all aircraft, though I can't answer for other airlines.

Shortly after a new ILS system had been installed at Sumburgh in the Shetlands, I checked the weather and decided to postpone my departure from Kirkwall, where the weather was good. I was hanging around the office waiting for better weather reports when I overheard Shetland on the phone saying that the Aberdeen flight had landed. "Who is the Captain? Put him on the phone!"

I spoke to George Florence who said that in spite of discouraging weather reports from Tower, he saw the runway lights right on the decide call using the newly installed ILS. I stirred everyone up, boarded the passengers and we set off. My co-pilot flew a lovely approach right down the radio beam while I saw nothing but cloud. But just at the moment he called "Decide" I saw the lights, called "Land," and we landed, just as George described.

In spite of what people say, the ATP had many good points. The cabin looked modern and attractively functional, its toilet was as good as in any jet, and it was quiet and fuel efficient. But for me reverse thrust on the propellers was a great bonus. I normally used a bit of reverse on the landing run to slow the beast down, mainly because I didn't like the carbon brakes. If used on landing they heated up and made taxying erratic as they began to snatch when hot. The result was that if I applied just a gentle touch of brake approaching the parking stand I found that one side would grab and the aircraft would lurch to that side. However, if I kept off the brakes on landing they worked perfectly smoothly when taxying in, so all slowing down on the runway was done with reverse thrust.

On one occasion it came in useful when taxying too. After landing at Glasgow, we shut down the left engine after clearing the runway and the ground controller gave us parking stand thirty-something, but I didn't believe him. We never park there, and I said so. He was quite adamant that we were allocated that stand, miles from the terminal so I headed there but asked the co-pilot to call company on the other radio to confirm. He took a while to get through, and they said they would look into it. I was just pulling onto this unusual parking spot when ground came back to say, "Sorry, it should have been the usual stand 18."

I asked the ground controller to send a marshaller, as quickly as possible, so that I could reverse out and proceed to 18. Soon the van pulled up, the marshaller jumped out and waved me back so I applied reverse gently to my one running engine and we slowly rolled back into the middle of the taxiway. The trick now is NOT to apply the brakes, as that can make the aeroplane tip back on its tail. Instead we cancel reverse and apply a little forward thrust to stop, then taxi forward to our correct stand.

I was rostered for an early flight from Manchester to Jersey and back, followed by Edinburgh and back, to passenger home to Glasgow the following day. I met the co-pilot, we pulled out the weather reports and other paperwork, and the co-pilot settled in an easy chair while I advised operations in Manchester to cancel the flight since Jersey was fogbound. They told me that all their Jersey flights that week had been cancelled, so could we please have a go, since the forecast was that the fog would clear. Our compromise was that they would put an indefinite delay on the flight, and wake me when the fog cleared. I told the two cabin-crew who lived nearby to go home, but wait by the phone. The crew room phone rang an hour later.

"Operations here Captain, I've spoken to our people in Jersey and they say the fog will clear soon so could we board the passengers now? We really would like to get a flight in this week and being Friday it could be our last chance."

I told them that as soon as the fog lifted we would go. But half an hour later, "Captain, I've spoken directly to the meteorologist in Jersey and he says the clearance is on its way, a clear front will reach them in half an hour. Please phone him yourself, here's his number." I rang the metman who was full of confidence that the clearance would arrive within the hour, and I began to soften when Operations rang again.

"Captain, time is getting on, could we get you underway soon, as by the time you get to Jersey it will be clear. We will put the standby crew on your Edinburgh flight, and you can just fly to Jersey and back. Can we board in 25 minutes?"

I told them to phone the cabin crew at home and bring them back, load fuel for Jersey with a Dinard diversion plus 90 minutes extra, then board passengers to depart in one hour, my best offer.

While I called Manchester for start clearance my co-pilot copied the latest Jersey weather, 100 metres visibility in fog. We took off and flew towards Jersey at economical speed and when within radio range asked their weather. 100 metres, fog. Arriving overhead we joined the hold and I called the company manager in Jersey to inform him, and he put me through to the world's most optimistic metman.

"What about this clearance you promised, for three hours ago?"

"Well," he said, "There is a front coming in from France behind which the weather is definitely clear and it will be here any time soon."

I hated to disappoint him but from up there I could see the edge of the fog, between Jersey's shore and France, and it was static. It was not moving, Jersey's visibility was still 100 metres, so after an hour I set off for Dinard in the clear bit of France. On the ground in Dinard I phoned Manchester Operations and liaised between them and the local French handling company, trying to get our passengers to Jersey. Operations suggested a ferry, so when is the next ferry? Monday. What about the fast hydrofoil service? They start again in Springtime.

Out of options, I loaded enough fuel to fly everyone back to Manchester, plus a generous diversion and set off. As we climbed out over the French coast I called ahead to Jersey. "If your fog has lifted I could still divert into Jersey, with you in ten minutes."

"Sorry, still 100 metres in fog. Have a nice flight."

Sixty disappointed people arrived back in Manchester, having wasted lots of time and fuel. At least we tried. I have to say that Managers never questioned any decision, whether it was the Jersey trip, a fuel load, or a decision to go-around (3 times, at Kirkwall, and another 3 next day) or a decision to land in marginal weather like at Shetland. I had heard of management in other airlines criticising Captains for carrying more than minimum fuel or asking for worn tyres to be changed, but that's not my experience in BA. There is an old (US military) joke about a pilot writing in the tech log 'right outer tire almost needs replacing,' to which the engineer writes in reply, 'almost replaced right outer tire.'

It was about this time that British Airways bought Dan-Air (for £1) following unsuccessful attempts to merge the failing airline with a healthy competitor. This time it really was a rescue. BA kept some of the routes, aircraft and staff but not all, and my seniority was not affected. Also about then, one of my mates from Budgies who had moved on to Boeing 757/767, had a drink problem. He ordered one drink too many from late-night room service on a nightstop, the hotel complained of damage done to his hotel room, and after the ensuing company investigation he was fired. His co-pilot was rumoured to have the perfect alibi, having been in bed when the late drinks were ordered with not one, but two stewardesses from the crew. Talk about an ego boosting happen-stance!

I had aunts, uncles and cousins in Canada, in both Vancouver and Victoria B.C., and just up the road they had a ski resort at Whistler. Now that I was into skiing that combination justified a trip. My wife and I flew into Vancouver on staff tickets, then used more staff tickets to take a chance on standby seats with Air BC to Victoria, on Vancouver Island. We were lucky to get on, and I was really lucky to be invited to the cockpit after showing my British Airways identity card. After explaining that I flew similar turboprops in Scotland the Captain said, "In that case we'll go the pretty way!"

After take-off we flew at a low civilian level (as opposed to wave-top height like Air Force pilots). We flew over the water and a few small islands and sped past the ferry, then approaching the main island he asked where my family lived. I told him the general area where an uncle lived and he overflew it before crossing the harbour where the small seaplanes operated and then on to Victoria airport where we were met by my cousin.

We stayed with her for a night then flew back to Vancouver where the bus departed for Whistler for a few days skiing. The last day's skiing ended with the bus to the airport and a disappointment. The flight was full. The British Airways 747 had not a seat left for us (staff are standby remember). We asked about Air Canada but their flight left earlier, so we had to find an affordable hotel in town. We spent a day in Vancouver after all, and met up with my other cousin for a coffee. Pre-warned by BA that they were full again, that night we asked if Air Canada would take our staff tickets and they were helpful and charming, giving us seats right away as the flight was only half full.

While taking our seats in the Boeing 767, my wife caught me ogling two very attractive ladies three or four rows in front. They really were stunning, but best ignore them. They disappeared soon anyway, maybe changed seats. Dinner was served, and devoured (not bad) and then after a while I asked to visit the cockpit, showing the cabin crew my BA identity card. I was invited in, and who do you think sat behind the two pilots on the extra seats? The two women who had caught my eye turned out to be pilots as well, both Captains on the Air BC Dash 8 fleet which had taken us to Victoria. We had much in common to talk about.

One topic was that the two 767 pilots had no relief, no bunk time, no heavy crew. I knew that BA carried one heavy crew member on the Vancouver to London, so I was quite surprised that these two had to stay awake all night and then do the landing at Heathrow. It didn't seem right. The only night flying I had really done at that time was Glasgow to Dublin and back, but that was easy. If we hurried we could be home by 3 a.m., like a late party. I spent an hour or two in the cockpit, then went back to see if could recline my seat and sleep a bit, leaving the lady pilots chatting.

Chapter 8
Longhaul on the 747

British Airways, or at least their bean-counters, wanted cheaper pilots on the ATP. They now had some fairly experienced pilots flying right hand seat on big jets, which made lots of profit and could afford expensive senior pilots like me, so they started allowing us to swap around. A young chap transferred onto the ATP, became a Captain and was paid a little extra. I decided to transfer onto the Boeing 747 as a very senior co-pilot, as I had never experienced longhaul or the top end of the Bidline. Being senior I could get the best trips and so I had a pay rise as well. The company paid for two conversion courses, paid us both extra, and saved money? I suppose I don't need to understand—just fly the plane.

The conversion course started like all previous, with the issue of a set of aircraft manuals, but we then split into pairs, a Captain and co-pilot. For the automated and computerised part of the course we sat in a cockpit mock-up made up using life-sized photographs of all the panels. We sat and watched slide-shows, one after the other, that explained how every system worked and what every knob and switch controlled and where to look for its result. When moving a switch, as pilots we had been trained to watch a light or gauge for the result of the change and ensure it was the correct result, not just blindly flick a switch.

We then used automated question and answer sessions that checked that we had taken in and assimilated all the information thrown at us. There was an instructor in general charge of the course who would answer any question we needed answered. In the end we covered every question in the CAA's database, and thousands more besides, so exam time was no problem. The CAA exams were split into four sections and were easy, but pass marks were high (over 90% I think). I managed to score 100%, four times (not that unusual).

The next stage of training was in the simulator, still working as a pair. The simulators were very realistic, even back then, and we used them to learn how to handle this enormous machine, fly it to its limits at the stall, high speed and high altitude. We learned how to fly on instruments both on autopilot and by hand, but most of the course was about handling all the emergency procedures, and failures of engines and systems, of which there were many.

This aircraft was the first jumbo jet (B747) fitted with a glass cockpit, following its success on the 757/767. It was far more sophisticated than the simple one on the ATP and took some getting used to. All the flying instrument information that we formerly gathered from a scan of five round dials was collected on a single square screen right in front of each pilot.

The artificial horizon is centre-stage on the screen, and to its left is a speed ribbon, a moving speed scale with high speed at the top, low speed at the bottom and your actual instantaneous airspeed highlighted dead centre. There is also an acceleration indicator, a speed trend, that tells what your speed might be in a few seconds time. Down the right side the same thing is done for height, a ribbon scale with trend and your actual height highlighted. And right of that again, on the screen edge, is the vertical speed scale. All you need to know is on one screen, plus a heading on a scale at the bottom edge, and along the top edge all the autopilot engagement modes. It is a lot to take in.

There is a second screen, inboard of the main screen, with the top half of a compass rose drawn, with your actual heading (accurate to 3 digits) highlighted top centre, your track drift marked and also the selected (desired) heading. The knobs to select desired headings, heights and speeds are on the autopilot panel on the coaming edge.

In the top left corner of the screen is displayed the calculated wind speed and direction, while the top right corner has the next track-point name with ETA and distance. Bottom centre of the screen is a triangle representing the aircraft position, with a position trend line, and between the bottom and compass rose a map is displayed electronically, with your planned route, radio beacons, defined points, airfields, and so on marked. You can also superimpose weather radar on the map.

A further screen, mounted in the centre panel in front of the throttles, displayed engine instrument information for the four RB211 engines. The display showed a round dial with a needle, which is great for seeing trends and for spotting the odd one out, and also a digital readout of the instantaneous number—whether a thrust, RPM or temperature. Another neat feature was that the colour of the number changed from white (normal) to amber (marginal) to red for outside limits. The same screen could be switched to show other useful additional information on various systems. Inertial navigation and the glass cockpit were really the only significant innovations I witnessed in thirty years.

Following the simulator course we entered the hall housing all the personal safety equipment, like life jackets and smoke hoods, and also the fuselage mock-ups with genuine Boeing doors that we practise opening and closing from the outside, then from inside in normal operations, and then we practised the emergency procedures for opening doors and deploying the inflatable slides that doubled as rafts.

Since the ATP I flew previously was a light twin propeller aircraft, I had to land an empty aeroplane before I carried passengers. Even taxying was a challenge. I had never sat that high. It was like driving a block of flats down the road while sitting at a fourth-floor window. We could not see the wingtips, but knew they were way out and back there somewhere. "If in any doubt," we were told, "Stop where you are and ask ATC to send out a leader truck to guide you to and from the parking area." Sound advice.

And with so many main wheels taking the vast weight of this machine, and very little weight on the nosewheel, turning had to be very slow and careful as otherwise the nosewheels would just skid sideways. With two forward and two rear main legs, each with a tilting four-wheel bogie, there was so much give in the undercarriage that acceptably smooth landings were the norm. The 747 undercarriage was so much more forgiving than the rigid posts on which the Trident landed.

This new version of the old Jumbo Jet, with the new fancy turned-up wing extensions, has a wingspan of about 211 feet (64 metres) and length 232 feet (71 metres). Typical passenger seating in BA was around 400, depending upon just how much space was used for Club and First Class. Its maximum weight on start-up would be a fraction under 400 tonnes, of which up to 173 tonnes could be fuel (47700 of the Queen's gallons). The wings were used as fuel tanks, there were tanks in the centre fuselage, and even the tail had been fitted with a tank, that held 12000 litres (2640 gallons). We needed a runway 3.2 km long for take-off fully laden, even longer at hot and/or high airports, like Nairobi or Mexico City.

The 747-400 was operated by two pilots (no engineer) but supplemented by another co-pilot on long trips, or an extra captain and co-pilot on really long sectors. The cockpit had 4 seats therefore, as on these very long trips all four pilots were present at take-off and landing. In general the pilot flying the sector (who did the take-off and landing) did the external check, unless there was a heavy Captain in which case he would do it. The heavy co-pilot would do all the mundane cockpit checks of books and circuit-breakers to let the two operating pilots concentrate on programming the Flight Computers for the route.

Just behind the four seats there were 3 doors, one for cockpit access, one to enter the pilots' private loo, and one to access a tiny bedroom with room for two bunk beds and one person standing up. Most of us partially undressed to sleep, in some kind of sleep suit, track suit or pyjamas. It was always possible to be called back to the cockpit for an emergency, and it wouldn't be appropriate to handle an emergency naked. It made visits to the en suite loo across the cockpit easier too, as in those days you never knew who might be visiting the cockpit.

Each of the two pilots has a defined role, which varies from airline to airline. In British Airways one pilot was the 'handling pilot,' who handled the flight controls for take-off and landing, the other obviously was non-handling. I'll describe what each did when the Captain was the handling pilot, but after training both were equally qualified and swapped roles on alternate flights.

The Captain did the walkaround while the co-pilot programmed the route in the flight computer and each set up his own panel. The co-pilot read the checklist and both checked that all switches and systems were correctly set. The Captain briefed the co-pilot on the SID route and procedures they were going to follow, then while the co-pilot engaged with ATC, the Captain would welcome the passengers on board on cabin address.

The Captain checked and signed all the paperwork, tech log, loadsheet etc., and that was never delegated. After getting the ready signal from the dispatcher (who removed the jetty), the ground engineer, the senior cabin crew, and ATC clearance of course, the co-pilot started the engines as the aircraft was pushed back. Occasionally we had to start engines after pushing back and applying the parking brake, as some tugs were not strong enough to push against four engines at idle power. The Captain taxied while the co-pilot ran the checklists and handled ATC.

On take-off the throttles were opened up to a low power setting (about 25%) and when they had all stabilised at this setting the co-pilot called "stable" then take-off power would be selected and when achieved the co-pilot called "power set." The copilot called "80 knots" for the instrument check, then "V1" and "Rotate," and after take-off "Positive climb," the Captain responded, "Gear up" and the co-pilot pulled up the landing gear lever and flaps on demand (after checking the airspeed) then read the checklist.

Thus the flight proceeded until about an hour before landing time the Captain handed control to the co-pilot and briefed him on what he wanted done and how. He went over the expected route and anticipated weather and, especially if the forecast was poor, he briefed him to fly on autopilot right to the minimum height, call "Decide" and then fly a go-around on autopilot unless the Captain had taken control to land by that point.

We no longer had a flight engineer so all the calls that he used to do were automated. The flat American male voice would call the heights, "one thousand," "one hundred," "fifty, thirty, twenty, ten." That's the wheel height above the runway. But a British lady chipped in to call, "fifty above," "Decide" at the pre-selected time. That's because British Airways had her fitted specially, as the standard American call was "approaching minimums." "Minimums." Not punchy enough: the "Decide" call was a command, difficult to ignore.

The Captain started the flare during the "thirty, twenty" and slowly closed the throttles on "ten," more or less. The airbrakes deployed automatically when the main wheels landed, the co-pilot selected reverse on the engines, and the wheelbrakes (mains only) were automatically applied when the nosewheel landed. These settings were selected during the briefing. For a manual landing the decide call was set for 200 feet, or much higher for weird approaches like the checkerboard approach at Kai Tak at Hong Kong or a Canarsie into JFK, but often the Captain (or whoever was landing) would take control and cut out the autopilot as soon as the checks were complete and he could see the runway.

Line training, with a training captain, to get used to flying the aircraft operationally, went well, although it did necessitate cancelling the family's summer holiday plans. After that I was free to choose my own trips from a privileged position near the top of the Bidline. There were still plenty of pilots above me, but far more below. The long trips that had extra crew on board attracted additional payments for those involved, and were less tiring than long trips that missed out on bunk time, so long 'heavy crewed' trips were very popular. They were the trips usually picked up by us senior pilots.

Apart from the extra money, we were never more than a few hours from a bunk. In addition to bonuses for long flights we collected meal allowances which varied from 'loadsamoney' in Japan and the middle east to not much in the USA and even less in Africa.

During a convenient break in my line training I received my first Bidline package, a weighty wad of A4 paper containing all the details of all the work trips available the following month.

My wife also managed to book at very short notice a brief holiday for the disappointed family, three nights in a luxury caravan in Aviemore. I spent much of the holiday trying to sort out my bid preferences. The lounge of the caravan was covered with A4 paper with multi-coloured highlights. A better way had to be found, and turned out to be available.

An enterprising soul amongst our community had written a computer program that ran on a PC. IBM were the market leaders then, and anything else was called "IBM Compatible." I bought an IBM PC, built down the road from me in Greenock. Programming the computer entailed a steep learning curve but was worth it. The Bidline was sorted easily and painlessly (and paperlessly) from then on.

Once I was cleared as an operational co-pilot, I took my first book off its dusty shelf, bought a laptop PC (another early IBM), finished my book, got it published and started a monthly column in a model aeroplane magazine. The laptop went away with me on all my trips and was used to write my magazine column. The book was a bit technical, about 'Basic Aeronautics' (my degree course) as it applied to model aircraft. The column, called Aerodynamic Forum, dealt with readers' questions about model aeroplanes, how they fly and why they sometimes don't. All of it was written in company time when stuck away in hotels abroad, except in Hong Kong.

The first trip I selected was to Hong Kong. I arrived early, introduced myself to the Captain and started with "I'm new, just finished training, and my previous fleet was the ATP in Highland Division."

To which he replied, "You'd better do the take-off and landing then." Remember, this was in the old days of Kai Tak airport in Hong Kong, before Chek Lap Kok was built. I'd better explain.

Runway 13 at Kai Tak had hills on the approach path making it impossible to approach it directly, so we used to fly in from the west, with Lantau Island rising steeply on our right side, as we followed a radio beam that took us straight on and down towards—a hillside. Nearing the small hill, whose rocky face was painted with a huge orange and white checkerboard, we had to make a gentle 45-degree visual right turn to line up with the runway and land. Typically we started the final right turn (the 'checkerboard turn') at a height of about 650 feet to end up at 200 feet lined up with the runway.

This was the procedure normally used due to the prevailing wind direction in Hong Kong. Due to the late visual turn in final approach, runway 13 was unusable in low visibility conditions. At night or in mediocre visibility there were lead-in lights to help guide your eye (and hence the aeroplane) from the checkerboard to the runway. All this was explained in a slideshow presentation by British Airways, which I had watched multiple times.

I replied, "Oh, thank you very much." and thought "SH*T! Thrown in at the deep end!" With an experienced captain to help and in good weather, we saw the checkerboard and runway from a good way out, the landing checks were finished and I took manual control in plenty of time. When really close to the checkerboard hill I lowered the right wingtip towards Kowloon's rooftop washing lines and the resulting turn took us neatly to the runway where I levelled the wings and landed. A bit like Shetland really, but without the lighthouse above us.

Over the next two years I did more Hong Kong trips than any other, some as heavy crew. It was a fun place, and the only destination where my laptop was not used. During the day we explored the shops and street markets, rode on the ancient tramcars, the modern underground railway and the quaint Star Ferry to Kowloon. I bought cheap computer parts and software from the myriad stalls in the Golden Arcade, attractively detailed blouses for my wife and my mother, cheap trolley bags (a novelty then), magic tricks and toys to amuse the kids, all kinds of things. A fellow aeromodeller gave details of some specialist shops where I often bought model aeroplane parts. I saw some wonderful solid rosewood dining room furniture at amazing prices, but it wouldn't fit my suitcase.

In the evenings we usually met in the basement Dickens Bar to use our 'free drink voucher' from the Excelsior Hotel, a ploy to keep our custom in-house. But though some ate in the hotel, we were in China and I went with the in-crowd who ate out. Out of many thousands of restaurants in Hong Kong the crew ate habitually at only a few. There was the Yin King Lau on Lockhart Road where they could seat six, eight, ten or more at big round tables. They started us with dishes of salted nuts and some beers, then they took our order. On the large centre turntable they placed 'the usual British Airways order,' multiple delicious dishes and a big bowl of 'special fried rice,' from which we helped ourselves after spinning the turntable for access.

This was normally followed by 'complimentary' banana fritters, and all washed down with a Tsing Tao beer. At the Mongolian (another novelty, now worldwide) we filled a bowl, they cooked it, we went back for more, they cooked it and so on until we had eaten enough, then went for another bowlful anyway. The Royal Hong Kong Yacht Club had a beautiful restaurant overlooking the harbour where they prepared excellent European cuisine, and they let BA crew in as guests. After dinner we frequented several bars and night clubs, including Joe Banana's and the China Jump where we would dance with the stewardesses who came along until the early hours. Did I say Hong Kong could be fun?

I also had a trip to Beijing (while we still called it Peking) and I saw the vast expanse of Tiananmen Square, full of bicycles and people. Next day I took a coach trip with another pilot to the Ming tombs, a vase factory and the Great Wall, which was particularly impressive due to its size and degree of restoration. There is an urban myth that it can be seen from space, but I am doubtful since when we passed over next day still climbing to 31,000 feet I failed to spot it.

On one of my Hong Kong trips in 1993 a strong wind was whipping the rain around the streets making shopping a chore, and when I returned to the hotel there was news that a Chinese airline's Boeing 747-400 had gone off the end of runway 13 into the harbour, and its fin was blocking the flightpath for other aircraft. The airport was closed.

Although the aircraft was partly submerged, all 396 passengers and crew survived. It transpired that, despite a bad approach, the captain did not go-around as he ought, and touched down more than two thirds of the way down the runway. The Hong Kong authorities, after reviewing the options, blew up the wreck, removing the obstructing tail fin, and the airport later re-opened. We went home a day late.

My next favourite destination was Narita, Tokyo's new international airport, because the money was good (no, excellent) and Japan was a novelty. The cabin crew were in a different hotel, not uncommon on longhaul routes. I spent half the day and half the night on the laptop writing my magazine column, but each evening I met up with the other pilots to walk or get the bus into town where we ate at three favourite restaurants. One was the Red Lion Pub, the other two were Japanese but with a Chinese influenced menu.

After dinner there was the "Flyers Bar," a nightclub/bar full of aircrew from all over the world, or the Japanese karaoke bar in town, while some met up with our cabin crew at the 'truck,' literally a big wheeled container on a vacant lot in the outskirts, with a bar and music inside. I tended to get the early bus back to my computer. There were other restaurants in Japan where I sampled the cuisine, but returned to none of them. I did not take to Japanese food. Once another co-pilot and I both ordered chicken curry and rice in an Indian themed place in Osaka. The waiter brought two bowls, rice and curry, and when we reminded him we ordered two portions he said, "That is two portions. You share." I visited a Japanese castle on one trip, expecting a great stone edifice on a towering rock, like Edinburgh, but it was a wooden replica of an ancient wooden fort, reminiscent of 'Fort Apache' in the wild west, with neither a hill nor a Samurai in sight.

I had quite a few interesting trips on the 747, including one to Caracas in Venezuela, though our hotel was on the coast away from the city. I took my wife and two daughters as it was their half term holiday week, and quite unusually we had five days off there. It was a rare opportunity for a holiday somewhere quite different from the norm. We spent most of the time in and around the hotel, which had a lovely swimming pool, though there were a few shops nearby, and a restaurant which did a flamboyant flambé, with great sheets of flame to the ceiling.

For some reason I flew out there with one Captain and back with another—and I was given both sectors. On meeting the return Captain I discovered that he had encountered all sorts of problems. His wife accompanied him on the trip and had had her handbag snatched by a pair of youths on a motorbike. She had been slightly injured when she had tried to hold on to the bag, but to no avail. Both their passports were the major loss, along with money, keys and other items. That dampened our enthusiasm for the place.

That Christmas I was again in line for a work trip so I chose carefully and landed a trip with four clear days in Harare, Zimbabwe, and took the family again. We lazed around the pool, soaking up the Christmas sunshine, and ate well either in the hotel or in town. We took trips in ancient clapped-out taxis into the city where I bought shorts, and we ate in a couple of restaurants, one being a Mongolian barbecue of all things.

The hotel laid on traditional Christmas dinner for the whole crew, seated around several large tables since many of us had brought family. The senior cabin crew member had three of his seven daughters on the trip, and I was seated opposite Chanel, daughter number five. The charges in the hotel were quite reasonable by our standards, including the extra room for my daughters (then aged eleven and fourteen) who were allowed their first experience of ordering a meal on room service, by themselves.

One of my best memories of the trip was the children's choir, from the local primary school. They all wore their whitest smiles and best school uniforms of white shirts or blouses and grey shorts or skirts and all had very neat jet-black hair. They were smartly lined up by the Christmas tree in the hotel foyer to sing Christmas carols in beautiful harmony. I'll never forget their rendition of "In de bleak midwintah," incongruous in the middle of equatorial Africa, in midsummer. On one of our free days we took our girls on an interesting mini-safari in a nearby reserve, but they were happy by the pool most of the time, and we ate lunch every day under one of the thatched umbrellas around the pool.

My younger daughter Sheena had a friend whose dad took her to Hong Kong on a trip and she often asked, "When will you take me to Hong Kong?" The company had a policy that children had to be at least twelve to accompany a parent on a trip. So on the first school holiday after her twelfth birthday I checked that there were plenty of spare seats, bought her ticket and off we went. First problem, our flight from Glasgow to Heathrow was unexpectedly full. I spoke to the Boeing 737 Captain who kindly gave us the two extra folding seats, but I had to check both my suitcase and briefcase into the hold.

After the flight, I thanked the captain for letting us use his extra seats and grossly overcrowding his cockpit, and disembarked with the passengers. We waited in the baggage hall for our bags, and waited and waited. Other flights disgorged passengers into the baggage area, and they left before us. I knew something was not right, so I went into the baggage office in uniform and borrowed the phone to call our crew room. I told the Captain about our delay, apologised, and suggested that I swap duties with the other co-pilot (who was supposed to be the heavy relief). They could get on with their briefing without me, and I would go straight to the aeroplane. Then I questioned the staff in the baggage hall about the delay.

Reluctantly at first, they told me that the redcap, the dispatcher in charge of ground operations for the arrival, had opened the baggage hold to retrieve a baby's buggy for a family waiting on the jetty. When the loaders arrived (late) they objected to his intervention and blacked the aeroplane, prohibiting any other members of their Union from going near it. I told the baggage managers that the evening Hong Kong flight would be considerably delayed if I did not get my bags, as my licence and passport were in one and I was not allowed to fly without them. However, pilots again proved to be an exception (as I hoped), when the Union officials allowed me to approach the leper aeroplane, open the rear hold and grab my luggage.

Despite the luggage delay, we both made it to our plane just in time for a scheduled departure. Sheena flew in the Club cabin on the upper deck, disembarked with the passengers and we met up in the baggage hall where she handed me a bottle of champagne (she is twelve remember). "Where did this come from?" I asked, and heard the tale of a Club passenger being asked to change seats to let a couple sit together.

Then he was given a bottle of champagne by the cabin crew as a 'thank you' from BA. He took it, as he didn't want to make a fuss or seem difficult, but gave it to the twelve-year-old he was now sitting beside, because he was strictly teetotal. Sheena didn't want to make a fuss either so took it and passed it to me as soon as we met. I think we put it back in the aircraft bar on the flight home.

I had arranged a twin-bedded room in our Hong Kong hotel so we lived in comfort for a couple of days, eating in the best McDonalds in town (well, she's only twelve) and spending a day at the Ocean Park theme park and the rest of the time sightseeing and shopping on the Island and in Kowloon.

Our return to Heathrow was nearly a crisis as Sheena, travelling alone on the passenger route between Terminals 4 and 1, was not at the rendezvous when I arrived (the long way round, via our crew room)! Should I panic, or just worry? I worried for several minutes, and then she turned up, seemingly unperturbed. She had taken a wrong turn, arrived somewhere unexpected, but asked a staff member who pointed out the correct bus to Terminal 1. That was a short trip when she was with me nearly all the time, so how would it be the next month when I took the whole family on a seven-day trip to Hong Kong, which included a day when I left them there to fly to Taiwan and back?

The long Hong Kong trip was pretty much drama free. I had booked a separate room for the girls, and we ate in McDonalds again almost every meal as they did not want to try Chinese food. The only reportable incident involved Hong Kong's underground railway the MTR, or Mass Transit Railway. The MTR was heavily used and often crowded. On one of our trips we headed down and onto the platform where a crowded train was about to leave. We rushed for an open door, I heard the ting of a warning bell and made a split-second decision to stop on the edge of the platform.

I was holding each daughter by the hand, but my wife Anne leapt onto the train just as the doors closed and it carried her away. The three of us stood there wondering what she would do, and would we ever see her again. I was the only one at all familiar with Hong Kong, so did she even know where we were going? With any luck she will get off and wait for us at the next station, I reassured our daughters. We maintained our position on the platform and boarded the next train, standing by the door in trepidation. When it next stopped, the doors opened, and there was Anne waiting.

On the day I went to Taipei and back my wife took the girls on the Peak Tram, and around some shops. We all did Ocean Park and I took them to my favourite model aircraft shop just off Argyll Street and bought a Japanese Radio control set saving 60% on UK prices, for them to take back through Customs.

One further advantage of living in Scotland while being London based was that the Scottish school holidays commenced at the end of June, a full two weeks before the schools of England broke up. That was fortunate because I could get leave at that time quite easily, flights were not as busy, and hotels were cheaper too. We had wonderful holidays at all-inclusive Caribbean resorts, though that first year it had to be cut short for a family wedding. At long last I bought a kilt, in Sutherland tartan, with all the paraphernalia. I have used it at many weddings since, especially of course those of my own daughters.

As well as the favourite trips I had a wide selection of the other routes on the network including Nagoya and Osaka in Japan, Jo'burg and Capetown in South Africa, Buenos Aires and Sao Paulo in South America, Los Angeles in California and Seoul and Kuala Lumpur in the far east, and so on.

On one trip to Mexico City I went on a trip with several other crew members to visit the mysterious Pyramids of the Sun, and the Moon, an hour and a bit's drive from modern Mexico City. Nobody knows who built them, but they were part of a huge city, said to be contemporary with ancient Rome. They were already deserted ancient ruins when the Aztecs occupied the region and ascribed to them the Sun and Moon dedication. I mainly remember an awful lot of steps up, and buying two shiny black deity figures carved from obsidian, a naturally occurring volcanic glass mineral. I also remember a pleasant lunch in a roadside restaurant.

We had an evening departure from Mexico City and I was the heavy, in the third seat. Mexico City, and its airport, lie in a wide shallow basin high on a plateau, over 7300 feet above the sea, where jet engines are not at their best. Added to that it is hot, and there are mountains around the basin, some rising to over 16000 feet. The BA office gave us the paperwork which included the local met office predictions for weather conditions at our take-off time over an hour later. They predicted that as the sun went down a wind would start up and the temperature would drop significantly. That let us calculate a maximum take-off weight from the manual, which we passed to the load planners along with the Captain's SWORD plus-a-bit fuel requirement. "No Problem!" according to the office staff so we proceeded to the aircraft and prepared.

After we were loaded, as the Captain signed the paperwork, the co-pilot copied down the latest weather, which was not good. Although the sun was down the temperature was not, and there was still little wind. We are too heavy to take off. As the extra pilot I was delegated the task of using the aircraft manual to calculate exactly how much temperature drop, and how much wind, or how much weight reduction would allow a legal take-off.

The Captain had a range of options. He could unload some passengers, not at all popular, or maybe some freight, but it was all perishable goods like fruit. He could unload some fuel, but that might leave us short and removing fuel takes time to arrange. Or we could wait for the temperature to drop as the evening progressed. The next half-hourly weather report showed a slight temperature drop, so his decision was to push back, start the engines to start burning off fuel, taxi to the runway and wait.

After waiting by the runway for half an hour or so, the wind had suddenly picked up, we had burned some fuel thus reducing weight slightly, the temperature dropped a couple of degrees, and I calculated exactly how much wind we needed for these latest conditions. Only fourteen knots would do, and Tower had just told a landing aircraft fifteen knots, right down the runway, we're in business! After a quick confirmation we had take-off clearance and we're on our way home, with all the people, bags and freight and still some extra fuel—in case.[2]

---

[2] Gwynn Mullett wrote memoirs called With my Head in the Clouds, published in two volumes, about airline flying with BOAC, and later BA. We flew together twice on the B747.

I managed to get a trip to New Zealand, after hearing that British Airways was about to give up the route. My flight stopped two days at Bangkok, then we flew on to Sidney. After a night there we flew as passengers to Brisbane to take over on an overnight flight to Auckland. We approached New Zealand as dawn was breaking in the east. The morning sunlight lit up the big natural harbour of Auckland beautifully, and the buildings were still surrounded by dark streets with streetlights, with only the roofs lit by a pale morning sun.

We could see the airport clearly from miles away, but were guided by the radar controller to the runway in use, where we touched down moments after the night curfew ended. That was the last British Airways aircraft to land in New Zealand, a poignant occasion, especially for the local staff. As the trip from Brisbane was short it was just the Captain and myself arriving at the hotel (the cabin crew had separate arrangements) where I immediately asked about sightseeing tours. "It's my first time here, probably my last, so I want to 'do' New Zealand today."

A couple of phone calls from a helpful hotel reception had me booked on a bus tour that would pick me up in twenty-five minutes, enough time to rush to my room, shower, change, and back down to board a half-full luxury coach whose hostess told us that to save time she would serve airline-style food and drinks at our seats, from the galley on the floor below, and whenever the bus stopped it would be go, go, go on the sightseeing. We stopped to see lakes, a working farm with demonstrations of sheep shearing and stuff, our hostess led an extensive tour around hot mud pools, smoking sulphurous holes and gushing geysers, "Nobody fall in please, we don't have the time!"—A Maori village exhibition (not inhabited), and caves where we were taken by boat to a deep dark recess to see the glow-worms. It all fairly whizzed past, hence the lack of names and details, and when we arrived back at my hotel the hostess woke me. It was dark and I had missed a good hour of the bus journey.

I slept well that night, and next morning the Captain and I visited the Auckland aviation museum where they had a great many interesting exhibits, including a complete Lancaster bomber from WW2, "Hey! Its wheels are bigger than the ones on our 747!"

"Yes, but it has only one each side."

Our trip home was as Qantas passengers to Sidney, then we flew the sector to Bangkok for a short stop then home. Auckland and back took nine and a half days. Then we wait forty minutes for the crew bus to become available, while the driver reads his newspaper.

I took my daughter Rona, aged 15 then, on a Narita trip, arriving after sun-up following a night-flight east across Scandinavia, and then the Soviet Union that went on for hours and hours. Previously I had no idea just how vast the USSR was or how many separate states it encompassed, but they all had radar and the radar controllers had good VHF radios and spoke good English, enough to say "Hello, you are identified on radar!" and fifty minutes later, "Goodbye, contact (the next state) on frequency…" We landed just after dawn, but to our body clocks it felt like midnight. After a bit of a sleep we walked into Narita town and looked round the shops, where Rona bought souvenirs, and we ate in McDonalds as I couldn't talk her into going local despite examining a few menus.

The following day we went into Tokyo by train. They said it would be easy but, although a few signs were in English, it was an unmanned station and the locals didn't speak English. We bought tickets from a machine but they turned out to be for a slow local train, not the express. The day sightseeing in Tokyo was interesting, despite the language barrier. I don't suppose they get many foreign tourists, the way London and Edinburgh do. Tokyo does have a big tower similar to Paris's Eiffel tower, and we ascended as far as we could. It was rather too hazy to afford great views. The train back was nearly a drama.

We looked it up, 16:14, platform 4 (at least the numbers are the same as ours), and trains arrived and departed frequently and punctually, with a sign a few minutes in advance to inform of the next departure. We stood on platform 4, our time approached, next train is at 16:13 to somewhere else. I sense an error somewhere, and it must be ours. Somehow, we discovered that there was a lower level, and upon investigating found that the level below also had a platform 4. We managed to get there as our train was pulling in. Phew, that was close! That evening Rona and I both ate chicken chow mien in one of the regular crew Japanese restaurants.

On the last day we left the hotel fairly early. On the day-flight west across the USSR we saw an awful lot of trees, an exceedingly big hole from which diamonds are dug, and a vast amount of empty space with just nothing, that far north.

Just before I was due to leave the 747 fleet my thirteen-year-old daughter Sheena had an urgent request. She wanted to see Universal Studios in Los

Angeles, therefore I had to get a suitable trip there during school holidays. The opportunity arose, her ticket was bought, and the day flight to Los Angeles went perfectly. Take-off from Heathrow was late morning, and due to the time zone change we arrived in the hot Los Angeles afternoon sun.

Now normally the crew would arrange to meet up at six for happy hour in the hotel next door, when a jugful of margaritas was half price and they had free snack-food, after which we often planned a meal at a nearby restaurant. However I never once made the restaurant, as by the end of happy hour (7 pm) my body demanded to be laid horizontal for an extended period, having some notion about the time really being 3 am.

With Sheena I had to make more of an effort, so after a quick change in the plush Sheraton Miramar we strolled around the streets, shops, beach and pier of Santa Monica and fitted in a meal on the outside terrace of an Italian restaurant. That's despite having been served lunch, afternoon tea and dinner by British Airways. It might have been a reasonable plan after all because, instead of waking at my usual 4 a.m., we managed to wait until a decent time for breakfast in the hotel.

By ten we were 'renting an auto' at the desk in the hotel where crew had a special offer, 27 hours for the one-day rate. At the rental desk a map was offered, on which the man marked the Miramar hotel and Universal Studios. I gave Sheena the map so she navigated like an expert while I drove, and we had a really good day out. Many good rides had been added since my previous visit.

The next morning I drove us to Long Beach for breakfast on the Queen Mary, an enormous liner built so very long ago on the Clyde just a few miles from our home. My father's uncle Jimmy had been a riveter in John Brown's shipyard and had worked on her. We wandered the decks, peeked in the cabins and then some exhibits in the lounges, one of which dealt with a tragic accident during WW2 when the Queens of Clydeside were troop ships. The Mary, with 10,000 American soldiers on board, was being escorted by the Royal Navy.

While they were zigzagging in case of submarine attack the liner collided with an escort vessel, a C-class light cruiser, and cut her in two. Both halves sank within minutes, and around 100 survivors were later picked up by escorting destroyers. The Queen Mary carried on at full speed, arriving in the Clyde (her birthplace) with a bent bow. The incident was kept secret during the war, but my father was a shipyard apprentice in John Brown's shipyard and helped patch her up for the return journey. The story went round that the off-watch Captain had emerged from the chart room asking, "What happened? I felt a bump." I told Sheena about the tenuous family connections, and we drove back to the hotel, returned the car by 1 pm. and had an afternoon nap in preparation for our teatime departure.

I had a skiing trip late that spring, and drove only as far as the Glencoe ski lift at White Corries for a change, instead of a further hour to the newer resort at Nevis Range. At Glencoe there were chairlifts, rather than an enclosed gondola, and there seemed to be fewer runs. The weather was fair and I had some good runs, though the snow was getting patchy this late in the year. In the middle of the afternoon, as I was skiing down a patchy slope, I froze mentally.

I was heading towards a small island of rocks in the midst of the slope and I found myself unable to turn. It should have been easy to edge left slightly to pass above the rocks, or right to pass below them but for what must have been only a second or two I found myself a helpless passenger on a pair of wilful skis that headed straight for these rocks like something from a slow-motion dream scene. The brain worked overtime but the muscles did not respond. I remember thinking that my next two trips on that roster were to Narita and Osaka, and I thought of the two thousand pounds in extra payments that I would miss as I lay in hospital.

Then I hit the rocks. I picked myself up and checked for broken bones or other damage. Nothing was broken, nothing torn or cut open, I got away with a few bruises, and I hadn't even broken a ski. Some of the frost damaged rocks had been splintered, so that's a headline "Skier triumphs over rocks!" I put the skis back on and made my way back to the hire shop where they were accepted without comment, and went home. I have never skied since.

On my last simulator check on the 747 I was paired up with another co-pilot, but because I was scheduled for a command course on the 757 they chose to put me in the left seat to act as Captain. The exercise started with an arrival briefing near the end of a flight to Hong Kong, with about an hour to go. We had all engines running and all systems go, a novelty for a simulator exercise, "what were they thinking?" I wondered.

But the weather situation was the tricky part, and of course they could still fail an engine or anything else at any moment, and we were sure they would. A storm was centred to the east of Hong Kong giving strong winds, poor visibility and heavy rain, and it was forecast to get worse as time went on. The tricky approach to land on runway 13 was in use. We passed over Canton, where the weather was good but forecast to deteriorate as the storm moved closer, and Canton was our alternate in the event of a diversion.

I was to do the landing from the left seat, sensible as the weather was poor, so I briefed the co-pilot to fly the approach down to minimum safe altitude. The co-pilot and I discussed the situation, and it helped that I had been to HK on numerous occasions. It was tempting just to land at Canton there and then as we passed over, but there was a chance of a successful landing at Hong Kong and that's what we were paid for. We were also paid to be very safe, but in the event that we failed to land at Hong Kong it was theoretically possible that we could perfectly safely make it back to Canton before the worst of the weather.

The usual approach to Kai Tak would take us high up over the city, then out to the east, followed by a wide clockwise sweep round to the south of the airport and then an approach from the west. I suggested that instead of that usual long route close to the storm we ask for a short cut directly from our position to a left turn onto the eastbound approach path. That would clear the high ground, save a lot of time and keep us away from the bad weather. The co-pilot agreed that it was a good idea, I called ATC (the simulator operator) with the routing request, which was approved along with immediate descent clearance. I called the CSD in charge of the cabin (the sim operator again) and told him to clear away immediately, prepare for a very quick approach and a bumpy ride and report back asap.

Meanwhile the co-pilot had skilfully accelerated the descent with airbrake and set up for the instrument approach using the guidance system that took us straight to the hill with checkered paint. As we turned towards it I asked ATC for a non-standard missed approach that would keep us away from the high ground and also the tropical storm. I still had it in my mind that the simulator exercise could go horribly wrong at any moment if we didn't get the landing. They let us fly down the approach with all engines running, but no view outside. Then, just as we reached the limit of the blind approach, the clouds parted and we saw the checkered rock face.

"I have control!" I announced as through the darkness I saw the curved lead-in lights in good time to follow them to the runway. I flew the arc round onto the runway where we landed in poor but not terrible weather. It was a bit of an anti-climax really, as the whole time we had been expecting engine failures, disastrous weather shifts and all sorts of calamities that never materialised. We held our nerve and landed normally. But it was only a computer game.

Chapter 9
Jet Command

I had applied for a command on jets, as a natural career progression, my first choice being the Boeing 757 in the Glasgow base of course, but there were no vacancies. I put as second choice, and was awarded, the longhaul base at Manchester which operated both 757 and 767 aircraft to New York JFK from Manchester, Birmingham and Glasgow and also Manchester to Los Angeles, but the LA service was withdrawn before I was operational. The Manchester base had been set up under political pressure to decentralise, and pressure within the company to set up low-cost local operations wherever possible. The result was a mess, operationally, with several pockets of crews operating to different industrial agreements, and my pilot group at Manchester was pay-capped, restricting career progression after a few years.

The Boeing 757 and Boeing 767 were two different aeroplanes. So that they could be grouped together for crewing flexibility they were built around the same cockpit. Once seated you could hardly tell them apart. The B757 was long and narrow, the B767 was a wide-body with two aisles and held more fuel, but pilots could swap from one to the other quite freely. Crews often flew a 767 into London and left an hour later on a 757, or vice versa.

The cockpit was similar to the 747 that I flew previously, and many of the control panels, knobs and switches were identical, or at least very similar. The course was structured in the same way with informative slide shows then questions and seemed easy as a result. I could afford to be more relaxed, take it easy, so didn't make 100% in the exams this time.

The B757 simulator course was very thorough, covering every anticipated emergency situation, but there was to be no base training. Since modern simulators were so good, my first landing in a 757 was with passengers on board. But since they didn't know, all the tension and pumping adrenaline was in the cockpit. That is still true, except that brand-new pilots fresh from training school still get half a dozen circuits in an empty aeroplane before carrying passengers.

One neat piece of equipment we carried was called ACARS, which was used for data communications, a bit like texting the office. We could send typed messages back and forward to company HQ, or to ATC to request clearances, we could get weather reports, and we could print it all out on a neat but basic mini-printer. There was also an automatic system for sending data to engineering back in London, and one of the parameters calculated and sent was the minimum tail height on take-off and landing.

When we pulled back for take-off (or the landing flare) the nose came up and, while the mainwheels were touching the ground, that meant the tail went down. If we slightly misjudged the speed or extent of rotation or landing flare the tail could scrape along the runway, doing serious damage. This is true of most big jets. We could go into the ACARS and request the latest tail height. If tail clearance was below a set figure it would automatically print a cheeky message to that effect. I often checked, but never triggered the auto printout.

Changing onto the Boeing 757 from the 747 was no big deal as the equipment was similar and we operated in such a similar manner, but we no longer had our own toilet, bunks or a heavy crew. My final check as Captain on the 757 was a bit of a nightmare, with the refueller spilling some fuel, some ATC problems and then a sick passenger whose condition worried the cabin crew.

In the end I declared a medical emergency and requested a priority approach, missing out the holding pattern, and I asked for paramedics to meet the aircraft at the parking stand. If nothing else it shortened the ordeal, and I passed the check. The medics who met our passenger said that he or she was fine to continue the journey.

My conversion and command course had all been on the Boeing 757, but before I could take up the Manchester based job I had to build up some experience on the new aircraft and then do the 767 differences course and ETOPS course. Although I had failed to get based in Glasgow, after my training I managed to get a temporary posting in Glasgow to gain that experience, which suited me great.

A few days after my final check flight I was flying from Manchester to Heathrow with Heather as my co-pilot that day, and the pilot of the small turboprop behind us in the take-off queue said there was a big hole in the back of our 757, a hatch or panel not closed or something. The implication was that we should leave the queue and go back to the apron to let an engineer check it. I reasoned that it must be the outflow valve, which fully opened automatically to prevent the aircraft from pressurising on the ground. If pressure were allowed to build up inside, the doors would not open in an emergency.

Heather looked dubious, unhappy, and had to be convinced. I shut down both air conditioning (A/C) units that pump air into the cabin for pressurisation, then manually selected the outlet valve closed and radioed to the pilot in the aircraft behind "Is that big hole you told us about closed now?" Yes it was, he said, and Heather was satisfied with that. I reset all the A/C switches to On and Auto, checked that the outflow valve had opened again and off we went.

One really windy day I set off on that same trip, Glasgow to Heathrow, to Manchester, back to Heathrow and return to Glasgow for the night. On each flight the wind became stronger. Leaving Glasgow it was just windy, and arriving in Heathrow it was uncomfortable, with turbulence on the approach from the big hangars upwind. The flight to Manchester was really bumpy, and on the approach to runway 24 at Manchester the ride was very turbulent, as it often is in strong winds. Just as I was starting to flare a gust dropped the right wing alarmingly close to the concrete, but I hauled it up level and landed. What a fright!

On the walkaround I stopped under the right wingtip and carefully examined it for damage! Nothing! I got away with it again. We bumped our way back to London and picked up the Glasgow weather. The wind had swung south-easterly giving a bad cross-wind on the main runway. Edinburgh had bad crosswinds, so had Prestwick, so I selected Aberdeen as alternate.

In contact with Glasgow ATC, the wind report they gave us had a crosswind (vector component) of 30 knots, and our limit was only 25 knots in those days. Prestwick and Edinburgh were out, but at Aberdeen the wind was lined up nicely with runway 16. We were allowed to make an approach to Glasgow, hoping that the wind would ease so that we could land, and though bumpy it wasn't as bad as Manchester. However the wind remained steady and so on reaching 1000 feet on the approach I had to go-around and divert to Aberdeen where we landed without problem.

The strange thing was that the twin turboprop ATP right behind me on the Glasgow approach had limits of 38 knots or so. He carried on and landed without a problem, and we could have too but it would not have been legal. A few years later British Airways paid Boeing for a higher cross-wind limit for the 757, up to 35 knots. Nothing was done to the aeroplanes, it was just a paper-work exercise.

After settling down on the 757 I learned what was different about the 767, everything outside the cockpit, and then, "Mind that step at the cockpit door, and see that fuel contents gauge for the big fuselage tank, that's different." But the big new thing to learn was ETOPS, and those rules covered both 757 and 767. If an engine failed on a twin engined aeroplane, the last bit of the checklist ended with the command to land, at the nearest suitable airport. It had to be within 60 minutes flying time unless the aircraft, and all its systems, and its crew, met a strict set of ETOPS rules. The rules were that the aircraft and its engines needed a proven reliability record, and electric and hydraulic systems had to have backups. Oh, and the crew had to know the rules and stick to them.

So these super-reliable twins were allowed to stray at first 120 minutes, then 180 minutes from airports. So we had maps with suitable airports marked, 2-hour and 3-hour circles around them, and we had to remain within the marked area—not a problem for the North Atlantic. We had a special checklist of ETOPS items, and I always turned up early to allow extra briefing time to do the additional checks. After a check flight to Boston I was cleared to go longhaul, so off I went to Manchester.

That is to say, I became Manchester based to operate the New York flights from there or Birmingham or Glasgow, but I still lived near Glasgow. I favoured Glasgow trips, but I could either fly on the morning ATP to Manchester or Birmingham or go down the night before. Every time I set off I ended in New York's JFK, the only variation was the departure point and I got to know JFK, and the shops and sights of Manhattan, pretty well over the next year.

British Airways had a new concept on trial in New York at this time. Every night they had 2 or 3 of our Manchester crews, 2 Concordes at least, plus several 747 crews, so they had bought a tall narrow building on 55th Street and converted it into their very own crew hotel. We called it the "Condo" (for condominium). It had about 25 floors with 3 or 4 rooms to a floor, and a reception desk and mail room on the ground floor. The organisation was (sensibly) delegated, to the small Irish Fitzpatrick Hotel group.

Winter came, not a nice time to be flying, especially in a twin, especially across the North Atlantic. On my very first trip, flying from Glasgow and still in Scottish airspace to the west, there was a KER-THUMP that jolted the whole aircraft. "What fell off? Or what did we hit?" the co-pilot and I thought simultaneously.

We scanned the instruments, one engine each side, burning, turning and generating. Everything was normal, but we were still alarmed. We were climbing, at something over 20000 feet, a bit high to hit birds but it can happen. No harm done then, but I had a thought and checked with ATC. "Scottish, has another aircraft passed this spot recently, we felt a bump?"

ATC confirmed that our track intersected the path of another large aircraft which passed only a few minutes previously, and was long gone. So it was a wake disturbance. I knew from previous experience that the vortices (whirlwinds) left by aircraft wings can keep whirling for several minutes after it passes, and by a remarkable coincidence that's what we passed through, a pair of old vortices.

On my next flight, also from Glasgow, someone took ill on the flight. The cabin crew all had first aid training so I asked the stewardess who came to inform us, "How ill? And have you called for a doctor on board?"

She didn't know but went to check, while the co-pilot and I compared our position to the maps. We are nearer Iceland, so we looked up Keflavik. The weather is horrible, but adequate, and the runways and radio aids are fine; we could be landed there in under two hours. After a while we had our answer, a nurse volunteered to look at the patient and does not think an immediate diversion is needed. But half an hour later, the patient is worse. Now we are nearer Goose Bay, and again the weather is adequate, and we could land there in less than two hours.

A hundred and fifty miles before Goose Bay we are getting close enough to talk to them, and I ask for an update from our friendly nurse passenger, as I need to decide now whether or not to land. At Goose Bay, by the way, it is about 25 below freezing in a fresh wind with blowing snow. No immediate panic says the nurse so we pass over Goose (thank goodness) and continue over Canada's icy wasteland down towards the US border and consider first Bangor in Maine then Boston for an emergency medical diversion. The nurse thinks the patient is improving slightly so we continue and eventually land at JFK as scheduled, but we were pretty tired out after planning numerous diversions on the way. The medics who met us said the patient was fine, just needed bed-rest for a couple of days.

I was off for Christmas and New year, and my first flight of 1996 was from Manchester to New York. I checked the weather in the crew room at Manchester with Todd Worthington my co-pilot, and we were not cheered up, not at all. The weather reports had all the ingredients for the script of a disaster movie, with a front moving up the east side of the USA bringing snow to all parts from Virginia north, from the coast to the mountains and forecast to go all the way to Maine.

The whole east coast would get snowed in. The only question was, how fast would it spread. I told Operations in Manchester the fuel I wanted, ninety minutes extra on top of Montreal diversion, the only place I could see that was not forecasting the snow. We flew a 767 with the big centre tank, so fuel was no problem. In a 757 that might have been difficult.

The flight across the pond was no problem, and down over Canada we pulled weather reports out of the ACARS. Bangor Maine was OK but snow was starting in New York and Boston. We carried on, fingers crossed. Reports showed the weather was deteriorating, but slowly, and the snow was moving north, but not as far west as Montreal, our guaranteed alternate. Getting close to New York we were told to enter the holding stack high above Long Island, during snow clearance operations at JFK. The whole east coast of the USA had heavy snow by this time, getting worse with every report, and we went round and round the holding pattern. After nearly an hour I called ATC. "Can you get me a diversion clearance to Montreal Mirabel, please? I'd like to leave in about six minutes." They acknowledged.

About four minutes later, "Speedbird, you are cleared for ILS approach runway 04R, take up radar heading…"

We had been in the hold for 62 minutes but were now on the way, though the radar controller was taking us on a long, extended routing. Then another weather report came through, the visibility was down again, about 800 metres. I changed my briefing. "We are on the only Cat 3 ILS in New York so let's use it. Fly me an automatic approach for a full Cat 3 autoland. We'll have lift dump armed but autobrakes off, reverse after landing but cancel if we don't keep straight on the runway." We could use as much runway as we liked.

The next weather report had another reduction in the visibility, to below our manual landing limits. Fortunately we were already set for an autoland, so we can continue even if it gets much worse. For a few tense minutes we continued the approach, programmed the autopilot for both a landing and go-around, landing checks complete, cleared to land by Tower. Outside, the landing lights showed a million snowflakes mercilessly hurling themselves at us.

Then, below the cloudbase, a sea of whiteness hove into view, with terminal buildings on the shore and lines of lights in the flat whiteness straight ahead. We recap our situation: a steady headwind straight down the runway, we're already cleared to land, the next aircraft is a long way behind. We let her autoland, let her roll, eased on the reverse, and she kept straight down the centre. By 80 knots we cancelled reverse and I took manual control, slowing gently and aiming for a gradual turn-off well ahead. We kept it rolling and taxied very slowly off the runway and cleared in plenty of time for the aircraft behind. Taxying to the gate was the next big problem, but it's not far, one of the closest to our chosen turn-off point. The airport closed 20 or 30 minutes after we landed, and stayed shut for nearly two days.

We parked at the gate, welcomed the passengers to New York and wished them a safe onward journey, and silently wished the same for ourselves. Our crew bus drove ever so slowly and carefully through the falling snow from JFK all the way into Manhattan and to the door of the Condo. It took a couple of hours. We checked in, and once in my room I turned on the weather channel on the TV to hear that this was the worst snow this winter. We met in the Condo bar where Patrick and Michael (Fitzpatrick staff) poured me a Guinness; I thought I deserved it. I returned to my room and the weather channel told me this was the worst snow for three years, then later the worst for five years, then ten.

In the morning they were already calling it the "Blizzard of '96" a once in fifty years phenomenon, the worst since 1947. There had been 20 inches of snow in Central Park, there had been power cuts all down the east coast, and fifty miles an hour winds reported. Very little was open that day, but I found a nearby pizza place. The following day, great efforts by the airport and city workmen had the airport and city getting slightly back to normal. That afternoon some flights operated in and out of JFK, but our schedules were in disarray. I operated a shuttle from JFK to Boston and back, and flew JFK to Glasgow two days later.

A month after New York's blizzard I was flying from there to Birmingham, a flight scheduled for 6 hours 40 minutes. We always had a tailwind going east, but this night it was better, stronger, than usual. There was snow forecast for the UK some time that day, so the sooner we get in the better. No delay in JFK helped, so as we closed with the British coast we eagerly copied the latest weather. There was snow down south and it was starting in Birmingham. We decided that East Midlands, which had no reported snow, would be our best alternate if needed, and were pleased to be given a quick approach straight in on Birmingham's runway 15.

Cleared for the approach, we were feeling confident despite the snow reports. After all, we are old hands at this, undeterred by a dusting of snow. But at around 12 miles on final approach ATC unhelpfully advised that the runway was closed for snow assessment. That was rather vague. I said, "Does that mean I should enter a holding pattern at the beacon GX?" and they agreed. So my co-pilot stopped our descent at about 4000 feet and entered the hold, while I called East Midlands for their weather report. The last half-hourly report was good, "But hang on, looking outside that's the snow just starting now."

"I'll be with you in a few minutes," I predicted.

Back to Birmingham ATC who had no good news, so I told them goodbye, I want to go to East Midlands, immediately if not sooner. They gave me a heading and a handover and I was being positioned for an approach by East Midlands, where we landed within minutes. Luckily we had looked it all up in advance so had all the information handy. Sure enough the snow had started, and was lying on the runway, grass and taxiways. I heard on the cabin address my cabin crew automatically launch into their cheery "welcome to Birmingham" cabin address, so I interrupted with the bad news. Birmingham is closed in snow, we are in East Midlands, and hours in a bus on snow covered motorways lay ahead (for all of us).

The flight time was six hours and six minutes from pushing back at JFK to parking, including the diversion. I would be most surprised if anyone had done JFK to East Midlands any quicker, so can I claim this as a record for an airliner? Less than half an hour later East Midlands was closed too, and the snow swept on up to Glasgow and Edinburgh.

That year my parents celebrated their golden wedding anniversary, and as a present I bought them tickets on Concorde to New York as BA were offering special rates to senior staff at that time, with return flights direct from JFK to Glasgow, though unfortunately I could not fit in operating their return flight. They had a great few days in New York, and the Concorde flight remained a highlight of their lives.

Storm in the Big Apple

"The wind blew as 'twad blawn its last;
The rattling showers rose on the blast;
The speedy gleams the darkness swallow'd;
Deep loud and lang the thunder bellowed;
That night a child might understand,
The deil had business on his hand."

Yes, it was a wet and windy September night in New York, with scattered thunderstorms, but the bard described such a night so much better than I can. I hurried the walkaround wishing I were somewhere else and boarded the 757 for a flight to Glasgow. Operations had warned there might be delays so we doubled the usual taxi fuel and added a bit extra for detours around weather. The Birmingham flight was scheduled to depart at about the same time, but we nipped in first for pushback clearance, and then taxi clearance from Ground. ATC read out the taxying route, the co-pilot read it back and commented, "That's the wrong way for that runway. They must be taking us the long way, all around the airport." And off we went. As we left the parking area the Birmingham flight was refused permission to start, they would have to wait on the parking stand a while.

Our taxi route led us after a few minutes to the end of a queue of aircraft. We wondered what the hold-up was, and then it slowly dawned that this was the end of a line four kilometres long, nose to tail aircraft all the way to the take-off point, queuing up for take-off. This would take ages. We could pull out of the line and go back for more fuel, but then we would be stuck like the Birmingham flight with an indefinite delay. If the delay were long enough we might go out of hours and not be legal to take-off at all. Now that our flight has started we can use our discretion, but do we have enough fuel?

The queue was stationary for a while then moved a few hundred metres, and stopped again. I shut down one engine which halved the fuel burn when stopped, but the downside was that more power was needed when we did taxi forward a bit. I told the cabin crew they had time to serve dinner before take-off, if they wanted. We recalculated just how much had to be in the tanks for take-off.

After a while it became evident that we would not have enough fuel. Progress was even slower than expected as ATC would occasionally suspend take-offs due to en-route weather. Outside the rain was lashing down and we saw lightning flashes illuminate the night sky, all around. Sometimes the pilot on the runway would refuse take-off clearance because of what he saw ahead on his weather radar, and the take-off point was still some way ahead of us. The queue advanced painfully slowly. When at last we could see the front of the queue, we were already right down to our minimum fuel for the flight. So near and yet so far, as the saying goes. So we did the only thing we could do.

We calculated it again, allowing for the lighter than planned take-off weight, and the potential to climb higher as a result. We could use a slightly slower cruise speed for economy, but the biggest saving was in changing the diversion alternate for Glasgow to nearby Prestwick. That gave many more minutes taxi time, and it began to look possible if the queue kept moving. The Birmingham flight still hadn't even called for clearance to taxi.

With only a couple of aircraft ahead, we restarted the other engine, and five minutes later were given take-off clearance, right on our new absolute minimum fuel. The weather on our route looked clear so off we went. We had spent two hours and thirty minutes taxying, from pushback to take-off clearance. The flight went really well and we landed in Glasgow with adequate reserves.

Glasgow-Based

My time in the Manchester base doing nothing but New York came to an end soon after that when I was posted to Glasgow, where I wanted to be. The Manchester posting had been interesting and I became very familiar with JFK airport, and the commuting from home in Glasgow had been tolerable. There were a few times I had to fly south the night before, and stay in an airport hotel. Once I had to hire a car and drive to Manchester the night before to stay in the airport hotel. But now I lived fourteen minutes' drive, sixteen at rush hour, from the car park at my new base.

The work involved many shuttle flights to Heathrow. They still called it the shuttle but the guaranteed seat and backup aircraft days were long gone. It was just another bookable service. I also flew several trips to Athens, the old airport, for a nightstop, our only foreign destination at that time. I was off on leave over Christmas and New Year, but with no holiday plans, just a family Christmas. Then Operations phoned to ask if I wanted a five-day trip from Birmingham to New York on overtime, arriving home Christmas morning, I think it was. But I turned it down, "You'll get someone else, I'm sure!"

A few days later, another offer. "We have another New York trip that Manchester can't cover. Five days, leaving Glasgow this time, getting back early on Hogmanay" (New Year's Eve). "Do you want that on overtime?"

I started prevaricating with, "Well, not really, but I've no definite plans that week so…" and in the background my wife is saying, "Great, we can all go!" So I took it. But I then had to rush to get tickets for the family (lucky the flights weren't full) and contact the Condo for a room for the daughters. They couldn't supply one, being full, but said they could put two single beds in my room if they removed the sofa and coffee table.

On the flight over, my Manchester based co-pilot confided that he had a relationship with a young lady in New York and would be staying with her, so my daughters could have his room. What a kind, thoughtful and lucky chap! The family had the evening of arrival, two whole days and we left mid-afternoon on the fourth day to land before dawn on day five. The weather was dry and clear, with good views from the Empire State building. On one of the days I was away on a Boston-and-back, but it was a great winter holiday that reminded the girls of the movie "Home Alone 2," set in New York, with its scenes of New York at Christmas time, including the big tree and ice skating at the Rockefeller Centre. They covered Saks, Macy's and Bloomingdales, with plenty money to spend (my overtime), and at my insistence we visited the Intrepid museum on my day off.

All aviation enthusiasts must, when visiting New York, travel west along 46th street in Manhattan until you reach the Hudson River, and there, incongruous in the cityscape of New York is the great grey bulk of a battle worn aircraft carrier, victor of WW2 Pacific battles and centrepiece of what even then they claimed was the world's biggest naval museum. The U.S.S. Intrepid is a must-see, with a deck full of interesting aircraft. Below decks it includes some space exploration exhibits since carriers recovered space capsules after splash-down. At that time there was a destroyer and a submarine to explore too, but much has been added since, including a retired BA Concorde.

Pilots in the Glasgow base continued to fly a great many shuttle flights, to and from Edinburgh as well as Glasgow, so sometimes I had to drive to Edinburgh airport and back. Most of our work consisted of these trips, but a few European trips including nightstops were mixed into the roster. Destinations varied from time to time. At first it was always Athens, then over the months and years other cities were visited, each one several times a month for several months. These included Rome, Stockholm, Istanbul, Warsaw, Lisbon, Nice,

Helsinki, Newcastle, Budapest, Oslo, Vienna, Barcelona, Munich, Prague, and Madrid.

One morning after a nightstop in Athens, as I led the crew through the terminal building, I was approached by a junior pilot and his stewardess girlfriend, who were hoping to travel on our flight and requested use of our extra cockpit seats if possible. I admitted knowing nothing yet of our booked load that morning, but wrote down their names from their ID cards and said I would see what I could do.

The station manager turned up at the aircraft with our paperwork, and a request that I seat two of his friends in the cockpit. I told him that I had already promised the seats to staff and handed him their names. He returned a few minutes later to announce that the young couple could not be found, so could he give the seats to his friends. The cockpit seats were mine and I wanted flying staff, because they spoke English, knew how to behave, knew when to speak or be silent, would not be airsick, and could conceivably be useful.

I told the manager to try harder, but after being told again that my preferred cockpit passengers could not be found I dug my heels in and insisted that he find them and get them seated behind me before departure time. They arrived in the nick of time and behaved impeccably, of course.

We had quite a few nightstops in Rome, with a few hours of afternoon and evening to look around and not too early a start. We pilots were in a very plush old-fashioned hotel near the Pantheon, but the cabin crew were in a different hotel on the outskirts. I did several Rome nightstops with Heather, a cultured lady who liked sightseeing, classical art and modern art. We wandered around the Pantheon, the Trevi fountain, Spanish Steps, Piazza Navona and a Gallery of Modern Art. I can't say I was impressed by the modern art. One exhibit in particular looked like some work that a bunch of builders had walked away from, leaving the job half finished, and I said as much. Heather was appalled by my attitude, but I enjoyed a quiet glass of wine and a meal with her in the piazza by the Pantheon.

The Lisbon nightstop was tied to an early Edinburgh departure in a 767. After our arrival in Heathrow we stayed on board and a new cabin crew boarded for the flight to Lisbon. The approach to Lisbon on a clear day was lovely, with great views of the city, the Tagus river beyond and the impressive suspension bridge known as the 25th of April Bridge. It was named after an uprising on that date in

1974. A group of army officers and the local populace armed with baskets of carnations deposed an unpopular government, according to local folklore.

Often we were cleared for a visual approach, hand flying downwind west of the city followed by a wide sweeping left turn round by that bridge over the Tagus for a landing on runway 03. The hotel was very comfortable with a few restaurants nearby, though it was a half hour walk to the city centre. Having arrived about lunchtime I normally walked into the city for a look around, and then back to the hotel to meet the crew in the penthouse bar to use our free drink voucher, followed by a meal nearby.

Vienna was interesting, and I took a tram ride to see all the old buildings, opera house, stuff like that, but cities with buildings, even old buildings, held no novelty for me. Prague had old buildings too, but the novelty here was finding a go-kart track in the basement of the hotel. I took my wife on a standover on which we explored the city, the castle, and ate in a lovely romantic candle-lit restaurant called the Palaffy Palace.

Later we moved to another more central hotel and I found two or three shops selling model aircraft. I even found a factory where a dozen workers were employed making model aircraft kits and parts, and I took home a large box from that trip. Warsaw was similar, but the old buildings were not old. I was told that the only building left standing after WW2 was our hotel, everything else had been rebuilt, including the quaint old square where the crew went for a beer and a meal in the evenings.

On one of the nightstops in Warsaw the whole 757 crew went out for a meal, except the chief steward, or CSD. He stayed in his room while the rest of us enjoyed an early dinner and of course the Purser and other cabin crew members started discussing him, and suggested we play a trick on him, as next morning was April the first. What to do though? Various hare-brained and totally impractical schemes were suggested and of course they wanted to involve us pilots to add a little gravitas to the proposed situation.

I told them that no way could I tell a tall tale and keep a straight face. It's just not in me, but I did think of a way round it. That involved using the ACARS terminal and printer which is used for sending urgent messages between the Operations nerve centre in London and all the suitably equipped aircraft in the fleet.

So next morning the flight went off as usual, check-in at Warsaw airport, briefing the crew—the weather was good, no problems or delays expected.

Passengers were boarded (just over half full). We started up and taxied out. In my initial cabin address I mentioned in particular that the route took us due west right over Berlin and on to London. In a quiet few minutes I manually typed out a message on the ACARS printer, just as if it had come from Operations in London.

A little while after take-off, the seat belt signs were switched off, the cabin crew commenced their service, and I summoned the CSD to the cockpit. I said, "This just came in from Operations, and concerns you," and I handed him the slip of printer paper without turning to look at him, as I made a show of being busy programming the autopilot. It read,

"Due to crew sickness in Berlin your WAW-LHR flight is to land in Berlin Tegel where CSD Gullible (not his real name) *is to take over in charge of the cabin on the delayed TXL-LHR flight and Purser Inonit will be in charge of the cabin when you resume your flight to London."*

He took the message, read it, swallowed it whole and rushed off to brief his cabin crew, who could barely contain their composure. They loved it, but ten minutes later I had to call a halt just as the CSD was about to announce the planned Berlin landing to the passengers. It would not be fair to involve them in the April Fool's joke. I have to say he took it in very good heart.

Our hotel in Stockholm was no longer city-centre, as in Trident days. Because Arlanda airport is a long, long drive out of town we had changed to a comfortable hotel nearer the airport. We missed out on all the big city shops and museums, since there was nothing near the hotel save a shopping centre with a small selection of shops and a couple of fast-food outlets. We could however go for very pleasant walks down by the lake shore past expensive looking houses, one of which had a seaplane parked in the garden. But that was it!

One winter's day it was dark already when I was landing a 757 at Stockholm, where it had been snowing, leaving a couple of inches lying on the runway. The hot runway lights had burned through the snow and were clearly visible. When on short finals I heard an aircraft behind, closer than I thought was sensible so after landing I asked for reverse but didn't touch the brakes. The controller asked us to "Expedite clearing the runway!"

"That's rich, it's his fault the one behind us is too close." Reverse gets cancelled around 80 knots, and when nearing the first turnoff I gently applied the toe-brakes—and we just slid right past that right-angled runway exit. It will have to be the next one then, that I had originally planned as it was a gradually angled turnoff, and we will turn off very, very slowly. I heard the aeroplane behind announcing his go-around on the radio and heard him roaring overhead. Sorry chaps, but in these slippery conditions nobody with any sense is going to expedite anything.

I set off one afternoon for a flight to Copenhagen. It was windy, all-over Europe, and especially in Copenhagen but within our legal and company limits, so no excuse to cancel. Every few minutes we checked the weather reports for Copenhagen and all airports around. They were all bad. The crosswind at Copenhagen was not too bad, as the wind was near enough lined up with one of the runways. It was just very windy, but still short of the company's 65 knot absolute limit.

There was nowhere else nearby that was at all attractive but we did have an alternate some distance away (I forget where) that was guaranteed adequate. This was going to be rough, and I was beginning to worry about the landing. Then, just when I was about to warn the cabin crew to expect a rough ride, the unexpected call from ATC, "Be advised that Copenhagen has been closed due to high winds. What are your intentions?"

A momentary private celebration, and then, "stand by!" We looked at weather reports. Nothing inviting, and though we had our alternate that would get us on the ground it was useless to the passengers. They wouldn't thank us for a long bus ride and then a ferry crossing in that wind. The ferries might be cancelled too. "I think Heathrow is our best bet, maybe half of them will get home to their beds." The co-pilot agreed, so we asked ATC for a diversion back to Heathrow, and that was that. I subsequently heard that the airport authorities had closed the place when baggage containers and other loose items started to get blown across the airport, causing damage. A wise decision.

I was pushing fifty when I first noticed that the cockpit reading light had to be on full brightness to allow me to read the approach plates at night. I still passed the medicals, but finally conceded that I needed a pair of reading glasses. A couple of years later my medial certificate stipulated that I had to have glasses, and a year or two before I retired I found that a pair of varifocal glasses were perfect for me.

The top part was plain glass for looking outside, the next bit once more let me see the copilot's panel clearly for cross-checking, the lower part made my own panel crystal clear while the very bottom bit was perfect for close reading.

They were also great for driving if I wanted to see outside plus read the map and satnav.

In the midst of all this shuttle and European work, in the summer of 1998 we were suddenly given the Glasgow to New York route, replacing Manchester based crews, but just for a few months. It was during that time when I was completing departure preparations in New York, and the last of the passengers were boarding, when a passenger popped her head into the cockpit to say hello. It was the wife of a good friend from Highland Division days, in fact I had known him since our courses at Hamble overlapped. She and her daughter had been given the last two seats, but my friend Andy and their son had been unlucky, and left behind.

None of the ground staff had even asked me about using jump seats for staff, so I contacted the dispatcher and demanded that they locate Andy and his son and get them on our extra cockpit seats, fast. Andy later became a Captain on Concorde and told me about the political stitch-up between the UK and French governments and the manufacturers that forced a reluctant BA to give up flying the Concorde following Air France's accident. He was one of the Captains selected to fly the last day's flights, the one over Stirling and Edinburgh and on down to Heathrow to land in turn.

I took my family on the New York trip again, this time in July, and it was hot. There was no room in the Condo for the Glasgow crew who were moved down-town to the Lexington Hotel, right by Grand Central Station. What a magnificent station! Rail travel must have been considered very grand when that was built, akin to air travel in my youth. My daughters needed their own room this time. We did all the usual outdoor tourist things, South Street Seaport, Central Park, Wall Street, the top of the Empire State building and the World Trade Centre.

Soon after that, the route was closed. The Manchester to New York was to continue, but Birmingham and Glasgow lost their links with the Big Apple. Other operators, like Continental from the USA started them up again and did it properly with a service seven days a week, and it expanded to Edinburgh with first one and later two flights a day. So Scotland benefited with a much-improved service and it was British Airways' loss.

Late in 1998 was the 25th anniversary of the graduation of Hamble course 721, and thankfully somebody in the course took the trouble to commemorate the occasion. He sent round emails to ask who would be interested, and the result was a well organised dinner/dance in a Sussex hotel at which almost the whole course attended, with their wives. Well done Roy, and others. Dress was to be formal, black tie, but rather than conform to the norm and just hire the usual DJ to blend in with the crowd, I decided to wear my kilt outfit with the formal accoutrements, Prince Charlie jacket, fancy shirt with obligatory black bow tie, sporran and brogue shoes. I was the only one of the Scots in our course who did so, and the kilt in particular attracted the attention of many of the ladies present.

In response to the obvious usual question I responded with the old music hall joke, "There is nothing worn under my kilt, it's all in perrrrfect working order." The event was a great success, but made me think. If only I had bought that kilt before Mick's one garment party!

Chapter 10
After 9/11

I was watching an old black and white movie on TV. Laurence Olivier played Admiral Lord Nelson, with the stiffest of upper lips, and Vivien Leigh was Lady Hamilton. Then the broadcast was interrupted with breaking news that an airliner had crashed into one of the Twin Towers of the World Trade Centre in Manhattan. After a few minutes the movie resumed, only to be interrupted again and cancelled completely when the second aircraft struck. We never discovered if Nelson enjoyed a long and happy retirement with his mistress.

That was the day when Americans discovered airport security, and understood what terrorism meant. Until then, security at US airports had been lax, baggage was put on flights without owners, and the IRA could openly campaign and collect money in New York and Boston bars to send home for terrorist purposes as long as the blood that they spilt was out of sight, an ocean away.

That cataclysmic event also sent a destructive Tsunami around the world's airline industry, as most Americans, and many others, stopped flying. The response from British Airways was to cancel many flights, cancel orders for new aircraft, retire the older aircraft prematurely to reduce the fleet, and cut staff. Of particular concern to me was the reduction in pilot numbers.

Recruitment stopped, but rather than make serving pilots redundant, the managers offered early retirement to anyone who was eligible (not me) and part time working to anyone else (ME, ME, ME). The deal was half pay for half the work, effectively the same two weeks off every month from then until BA wanted to change it, or for those of us within about 3 years of retirement, the deal was from then until retirement. The carrot was that our pension entitlement would be unaffected, the additional contributions being made by BA.

I had been scheduled for a conversion course back onto the B747, as Captain, a few months later. I rang the 747 manager's office and told them that I wanted the part time deal. Not during a conversion course, they said, and part-time would not be appropriate for a year after that during the settling-in period. Then we will see, but who knows? The offer might be withdrawn. I visited my current manager on the B767 fleet, a chap I had known since he occupied the room next to mine when our Hamble courses overlapped. I posed the question, "If I withdraw from the 747 course in a couple of months, could I take up the part time working offer on this fleet?"

"With effect from tomorrow if you like!"

"Make it the end of the month and you have a deal," I decided.

And so the following month I halved my pay and my work schedule, giving me much more leisure time, and crucially my pension was unaffected. I had the middle two weeks off every month, giving me for the very first time in my working life the ability to plan social events well into the future. Previously if I wanted time off well in advance for a wedding, dinner party or theatre visit, I would have to book a week's leave to cover it. An added bonus was that I was more senior on this fleet and so had a better choice of work, but against that we had no really lucrative trips. I chose my trips by how easy they were to commute to Heathrow, and how interesting.

The pilot base at Glasgow closed forever and thus I became a London based Captain on the 757/767 flying with London based cabin crew. They were very good, but I soon discovered that I could not take them for granted as I had the Glasgow based stewardesses. On one trip to Edinburgh on a beautiful clear day with little other traffic around we were offered, and accepted, a visual approach onto runway 07, the nearer end of the two. We turned on the seatbelt signs to give the cabin crew the usual notice and enjoyed the view. I adjusted the flightpath to take us over a model aeroplane flying site that I knew, but we were too high to spot any activity.

As we approached the centreline of the runway, still six miles away, the chief stewardess, whom we were expecting to appear with a thumbs up, threw open the door and asked breathlessly, "How long to go?" and I told her three minutes. "Not enough, can you extend?" she asked. An additional three minutes would do, so I asked ATC if I could make a left-hand orbit and they agreed. There was no traffic close behind. Instead of turning right onto the runway centreline as planned, we passed through it and then started a gradual left turn the long way round to end up on the centreline seven miles out a few minutes later. Then we dropped the wheels, and landing flaps, we finished the landing checks and the stewardess came in with her cabin secure check and a thank-you. We would never have caught out a Glasgow crew like that as they were so used to shuttle-length flights.

The trips that suited me best were trips to East Africa, in that they started late in the day, giving plenty of time to get to London on quiet flights. We flew overnight with rest time in a bunk, to Nairobi, Dar es Salaam, Entebbe or Lusaka where the time zone change was small. After two or three nights in the hotel we flew home in daytime, acclimatised to local time and daylight, arriving in London in plenty time to catch a flight home to Glasgow. Nassau in the Bahamas made a nice change too, especially as it involved a shuttle flight to Grand Cayman in the middle with a day off either side.

Grand Cayman was only an hour and twenty minutes away but we had three hours on the ground, with lunch provided for the crew in the airport restaurant. Popping over to Grand Cayman from Nassau made a nice little lunch outing. We felt like the toffs with their private jets.

The other great trip was the double New York out of Manchester. The Glasgow and Birmingham to New York flights had been withdrawn in 1998 and the Manchester flight was now operated by Heathrow crews as a seven-day trip. Day one was passenger to Manchester (easy from Glasgow), then we had a day flight to JFK airport New York, 24 hours off in Manhattan, a night flight to Manchester arriving breakfast time, 24 hours off in Manchester, and then the same again arriving in Manchester once more on the seventh morning to catch a flight home to LHR or Glasgow. I enjoyed resuming my affair with New York, its sights and atmosphere, but the model aircraft shop I used to frequent had moved, and was a shadow of its former glory.

We operated to Detroit as well, from Heathrow. Detroit airport seemed vast with five or six runways (Heathrow has two). But the international terminal for foreign airlines where we parked was incredibly tiny, with just three or four parking stands. The crew disembarked last and joined the end of a very long queue at immigration where everyone was scrutinised and questioned (just after 9/11 remember). It always took ages, but on one occasion a steward was invited into a side room. The rest of us passed through eventually, and we waited on the crew bus for him, and waited.

After a while, search parties were sent, in case he couldn't find the bus, local BA staff were questioned but had been told nothing. After more than an extra hour of waiting he appeared, and was not pleased. His name had come up in their computer as a known terrorist. There was absolutely no resemblance to the alleged terrorist, but they went through interminable checks on him and his background. The bit that convinced me we were dealing with clueless amateurs was that he had undergone exactly the same fiasco three days previously, and at that time had told them, "I will return in three days' time, write all this down and be ready!"

The contrast with East Africa could not be more stark. We parked outside the terminal building, over which was hung a big banner saying, "Welcome to Entebbe" (or was it Dar es Salaam?). We disembarked in shirt sleeves, strolled in through any open door to the terminal where all the black faces, including the uniformed security personnel, had big white smiles and we were greeted in Swahili with "Jambo! Habari?"

Our suitcases were waiting beside the luggage belt, or had already been collected for transfer to the crew bus. I generally took a large case for my computer, paperwork and reference books as I was still writing two differently themed columns in two monthly model aeroplane magazines.

In Dar es Salaam we often ate in the hotel restaurant, taking a taxi to town just occasionally. In Lusaka the hotel food was good, but we did frequent a couple of restaurants in town and a night club. After landing in Entebbe airport on the shore of Lake Victoria, we were driven in the crew bus to our hotel in Kampala, the Ugandan capital, where the crew frequented several good restaurants. I remember an Italian and two or three that served very good Indian style curries, and there was a nightclub. Some of the crew took a boat ride on the lake to Ngamba island chimpanzee sanctuary, but I had articles to write.

We noticed some alarmingly large birds nesting in trees near the hotel and they could be seen circling over the lake, worryingly near the airport. Fortunately they flew singly, not in flocks, as one of those could have made an awful mess of an engine. None of us ever hit one, but it would have been survivable (for us, not the bird). On one of our regular checks I asked them to try us with a worst-case scenario in the simulator, and that cheered me up.

My first Christmas in the London base was destined for a trip away so I chose Entebbe, hoping for as good a time as we had enjoyed in Harare. I planned to take the family but my wife was not able to go so I went alone. As it turned out nobody else on the crew had brought family so we had a quiet Christmas. The hotel again laid on a splendid dinner, for which we all sat around a large table under a thatched cover in the outdoor restaurant. Oddly, the senior stewardess had brought her own brussels sprouts. On other evenings we ate out in some of the lovely restaurants of Kampala. There is something to be said for a hot Christmas by the pool. Crisp and snowy is good too at Christmas, but don't you get depressed by dull and wet?

A year before I retired from the airline, on one of my regular February holidays in Florida, I just turned up at Kissimmee airport. I arranged for a flight in their US Navy yellow liveried, 1945 vintage, 42-foot wingspan tail-dragger with a big round 600 hp Pratt & Whitney aircooled radial in front (quote "the best machine ever built to turn gasoline into noise."). My instructor, John Hedgecock, showed me round this SNJ6 Texan, known in Britain as the Harvard.

I jumped up on the left wing-root and climbed into the front cockpit. John told me to fasten the parachute harness firm, not tight, (I need a parachute???) and then the seat harness. Then he ran through how to bail out. Undo only the seat harness, reach across with your right hand to slide back the canopy, and get out any way you can. "If I shout, **'bail out,'** don't ask why, just go!" he warned. Last time I wore a parachute, or flew in a tail-dragger, I was eighteen!

Then he explained the controls. Elevator and aileron on the joystick, rudder and toe brakes on the pedals, throttle in the left hand, and beside it RPM and mixture controls. Hydraulics lever, gear, flaps and carb heat on the left, radio switch on the throttle. But he had a duplicate set in the rear cockpit, so he would do all that and my set would move with his. The instruments were basic, as all the gyros had been deactivated as they don't like being upside down a lot (sounds promising).

John started the engine (yes, it IS noisy) and we put on our padded headsets which kept out much of the noise and allowed us to communicate. After the engine had warmed up he taxied past their Bell 47 helicopter (which also does rides) and out between the lines of parked aircraft then handed over to me. It has a steerable tailwheel linked to rudder, so it is quite easy, but you can't see forward past the engine so I had to zig-zag all the way to the take off point where we stopped for engine checks (oil temperature and mag drops) and take off clearance from the tower.

At 500 feet I took control and had a gentle waggle to feel them out. It feels quite lively and light on both aileron and elevator, but then it weighs a paltry two-and-a-bit tons. A little squeeze on the sensitive rudder was needed to keep the ball in the middle and avoid side-slipping. I adjusted the elevator and rudder trims to take off the load and climbed on up at 100 mph as ordered. On the way we made some small turns and John pointed out some landmarks, the lake, the highway, a small brushfire—even in February. In summer their smoke poses a serious visibility hazard. All the while he handled the throttle as he says these old round engines need careful handling as they are easily upset (unlike a modern Rolls Royce RB211).

We levelled at 6000 feet above an occasional scattered puff of cloud and I practised turning left and right, then some steep turns pulling a couple of 'g.' From there we progressed to wingovers where you dive, climb steeply, roll 90 degrees, and just let the nose fall sideways into another dive before rolling and pulling to recover.

"Let's try a stall and recovery—it normally drops a wing, usually the right one." John eased off the power, dropped the gear and flaps while I kept the nose up and the speed bled off. The controls became all vague, the nose sagged and the right wing dropped. I squeezed on some left rudder and moved the stick straight forward while watching the airspeed increase and then eased out of the dive. The wheels and flaps came back up and we moved on to aileron rolls.

Following instructions I dived the speed up to 160, then pulled the nose well up, eased off the elevator and pushed the stick hard left. The horizon whipped round, the whole world turned upside down and kept going round, then as the view became more normal I centred the stick. The nose was down a bit, and left of where it started but—hey—let's do THAT again. After another roll left and one to the right it was time to head back as I'd paid for only half an hour. (Incidentally, I tried that again in the last few minutes of a session in the Boeing 767 simulator, and it turned out OK, but don't tell BA management.)

I dived the height off and pointed in the desired direction and gradually Kissimmee airport came clearly into view. I flew a visual circuit join which brought us over the touchdown point at 1000 feet where John took control, dropped the flaps and wheels and flew a tight right circle back round to land. I taxied it back in where there was another volunteer waiting for a flight with him.

I didn't have a chance to chat after the flight and I didn't buy the offered video, but I still remember it all, especially the world whirling round in that front windshield. No gyros used, never mind triplex computers—that's REAL flying.

Summer Holiday time again, just the wife and I, and for something completely different we bought staff tickets to fly to Barra, at the south end of Scotland's Western Isles chain. The 19 seat Twin Otter was full out of Glasgow, with half the seats occupied by mail and newspapers so we flew to Benbecula further north and caught the southbound Twotter to Barra. We were flown, at only 800 feet, from there to the landing on the beach at Barra, a unique experience. Barra is said to be the only licensed airport in the world to use a beach. But what a beach!

Almost a square mile of level fine white sand that is covered by a foot or two of water at high tide, and dries out to hard packed wet sand for most of the day. The airline's scheduled times are subject to tides. The airport manager starts his day as the tide recedes from his runway. He drives out in a truck to clear the beach of any bunches of seaweed, floating logs or other flotsam that the tide left behind, then he opens the control tower and operates the radio to welcome the incoming aircraft. He also chocks the wheels and unloads the bags. I can recommend the Barra experience to anyone bored with the same-old airport tedium and queues, it is like winding the clock back ninety years. My wife commented that there seemed to be more shops on our Caribbean cruise ship than on Barra (she missed her department stores). "But there were twice as many people on the cruise ship as on Barra." I reminded her.

On the first evening of one memorable trip to Lusaka I had the crew round to my room for a drink, as the Captain was always given the biggest room. We then adjourned to the bar which had a karaoke machine, using which two of the girls performed a surprisingly good rendition of "Wind Beneath my Wings." We also met up with the BA station manager in Lusaka who introduced us to a couple of English businessmen, neither of whose names matter but I'll call one of them Richard Head, or Dick when we got to know him. They accompanied us at dinner and then on to a local night club where we had a great time dancing the night away.

One of the best aspects of East Africa is the small time zone change relative to London, just a couple of hours, and it extends the evening rather than curtailing it. However a couple of hours past midnight I was feeling tired, so when one of our karaoke girls, whom I'll call Elaine, said she was going back to bed I volunteered to get a taxi with her, hoping I looked protective rather than just knackered.

The following day I spent an hour by the pool and the rest in my room writing my magazine column but I met up with the crew again for dinner in the hotel followed by a drink and an early night, but I remember an altercation between businessman Dick and my co-pilot Iain, who offered to punch his lights out. It came to nothing however, not while I was around. Then on the third and final night nobody met up anywhere except Iain, Elaine and myself who went somewhere local for dinner, during which I heard a tale of crew relations worthy of a soap opera, some of it from Iain, some from Elaine.

Most crew members had fallen out with each other because Jane had slept with John, and that upset Jean who was jealous. Then Joanne had slept with Jim, but worst of all was Janet who slept with Dick, and nobody would speak to her afterwards, and so on it went involving almost the whole crew. I had the most incestuous cabin crew ever it seemed.

I began to probe for details, and as details were coaxed out, some from Iain and some from Elaine, of who said what when and to whom, among us we teased apart the web of innuendo, rumours and lies that entangled the rest of the crew. We began to realise that all the salacious rumours could be traced back to Dick. It became apparent that there was no evidence that any of the crew had slept with anyone else, least of all Dick, and Janet's reputation had been blackened unfairly. On the flight home next day Elaine explained it all to the crew and they were all friends again. I made up the names by the way.

I flew several trips to Caracas in Venezuela, and again we used a different hotel from last time. It had all the modern conveniences, like computers with internet access. Again the hotel was near the coast, not inland by the city, probably for crew safety. The crew did go out at night for meals in some recommended restaurants in the vicinity, but always by taxi there and back. The meals and wine were very good as I remember, but it was not a place to take the family.

Once a week the flight to Caracas carried on to Bogota in Colombia, renowned (or infamous) for its association with the illegal drugs trade. Bogota is a vast city, with over seven and a half million people (now), over ten million in the metropolitan area. The city and its airport sit just four and a half degrees north of the equator, but way up high in the mountains. Over a thousand feet higher than Mexico City, Bogota sits at 8660 feet or 2640 metres above the distant sea level. That is the highest airport used by British Airways and, unlike Mexico City's shallow bowl, the mountain ranges tower above Bogota all around, making Mexico City look almost ordinary. Pilots have to be extremely careful flying into and out of such a place.

Needless to say I watched the BA slide presentation many times, studied the maps, and learned the escape routes to use should we have an engine failure at any point en route or on the approach or departure. I had studied it way back on Tristar, and it didn't look any easier now, in a twin. I was in command now, and in the event of engine failure we had only one Roller RB211 to get us out of trouble.

We carried our ground engineer from Caracas, because the service was just once a week and engine starting at such high altitudes was problematic. The other difficulty with high altitude airfields is the speed. Aircraft instruments read indicated airspeed, which is compensated automatically for air density. But our actual speed through the air, and hence over the ground, is much higher where air density is reduced. And up there it is well reduced.

Another fifteen hundred feet and we'd be wearing oxygen masks. When flying visually relative to the ground we have to judge speed, distance, angles, closure rates and so on. At higher speeds than we are used to it takes a bit more care. The short stop at Bogota was uneventful and our engines both started first time, with a little flattery and coaxing from the engineer and ourselves.

My last trip ever was to Entebbe. On the way home my crew presented me with a card signed by them all, and a memento of Uganda. It was an unexpected and thoughtful bonus, and my mind wandered back thirty years. Throughout my career I found it easy to get on with everyone among both flight crew and cabin crew (with one or two notable exceptions, out of thousands). In fairness to the BA management on the 757/767 fleet, I again have to say that I was never once questioned about my carriage of additional fuel above the computer calculation, or any other command decision.

All things considered the job suited me just perfectly. I could not imagine doing anything else other than fly aeroplanes. And I never fancied the extra money and problems associated with being a pilot-manager. I never applied for a training job since, though the extra money would be nice, I didn't want the extra hassle and I didn't think I was good enough anyway.

I filled in the aircraft's Tech Log, EBB to LHR, Entebbe in Uganda to London Heathrow, flight time 9 hours 12 minutes from start of taxi to applying the parking brake, nil defects to report, a goodly but not excessive amount of fuel remaining. I signed it, for the last time. What a sense of relief. I had finally done it. Nothing could now go wrong and get between me and a comfortable retirement. I had flown thousands of hours, millions of miles, and got away with it. I had no scratches on the paintwork, not even a burst tyre, and in a couple of days my fifty-fifth birthday compelled me to retire from British Airways. That achievement took a long time and cost a lot of effort, but it's worth it.

A few weeks later, on a winter vacation in Florida, I sat in a Piper J-3 Cub floatplane on Lake Jessie, Winterhaven. This aeroplane was the simplest I had been in. It had a 4-cylinder 85 hp engine, and controls consist of joystick, rudder pedals and throttle. There were no flaps, electrics, lights, starter or radios, just two headsets inter-connected by a wire to keep out noise and allow us to talk. Airspeed in mph, engine rpm, altitude in feet (set to zero on the lake), and a vague magnetic compass tell all you need to know. I couldn't even see the instrument panel from the rear seat anyway. Quite different from the airliners I was used to flying!

After starting the engine by flipping the propeller from behind with his right hand, while keeping a firm grip of the fuselage with his left, while standing on the right float, Maurice my seaplane instructor slipped into the front seat as we started to taxi—there is no parking brake on a seaplane! He talked me through my first water take-off. Full throttle, full up elevator to hold the front of the floats well up. As the airspeed passes 25 mph, I release the back pressure on the stick as instructed, the nose drops to level and the aeroplane accelerates as it planes on the step. After a short time the ride suddenly becomes smoother—my first ever water take off! At 500 feet I backed off the power from 2500 rpm to 2300 and flew level at 60 mph towards another lake a few miles away and set up for an approach.

There is nothing to it, as there are no flaps or wheels to lower. Point into wind, going by the faint wind-streaks on the water, back off the throttle and wait as the houses around the lake get closer. We pass over the trees at the water's edge, I begin to ease back on the stick as I sense the water getting near, but Maurice says, "Down a bit more." I am used to big jets and have to steel myself to carry on down. Eventually, just as my bottom was about to hit the water, he tells me to check back, the descent slows, and we splash down with a little bump. After touchdown, full up elevator is like slamming on the brakes. The nose comes right up, the tail ends of the floats dig in and the speed dissipates quickly.

At a slow taxi speed Maurice said, "Lets change places, I'll climb onto the float and you slip into the front seat." That's a better view! I can see the instruments now, and it's less windy as well. I can see the fuel gauge too, right in front of me. It's a bit of wire sticking up through the fuselage top, with its bottom end in a float in the petrol tank.

Maurice told me about the CARS mnemonic for the all-occasions checklist. C is carb heat, off for take off and on for landing. A is for Area, the air and water area must be clear of obstacles. R is for water rudders, always up except for slow taxying. S is for stick, to remind me to hold it back at the start of take-off. Not much to it really, compared to the big yellow book in a Boeing. From the rear seat Maurice could pull a wire to lift the rudders at the rear of the floats out of the water. They must remain up during launching, flight, take off, landing, and all fast taxying.

A few minutes after another take-off we set up for another touchdown on another lake, and this time it was a touch-and-go. After touchdown, instead of hauling full up for the braking effect I had to open the throttle, hold the nose up just slightly to stop a slight porpoising, and we took off again.

The flight continued, from one lake to another until I completely lost count of the number we visited, and we never climbed above 500 feet. Most were touch and goes but sometimes we slowed down for a look around. By the time I had flown enough and we taxied into the slipway, an hour and forty minutes had flashed past.

Though I would dearly love to keep one of these little Cubs as a pet, I decided to stick to model aircraft but visit Jack Brown's seaplane base in Florida again in my retirement years.

Chapter 11
And This Is Now

I have regularly watched "Air Crash Investigation" on television. Though the programs have too much hype, too much screaming, too much shock/horror and too much repetition, I like the detective content. I am always looking for a divergence point, a point in the story where I would have done something different that might have avoided the crash. Sometimes there is nothing any pilot could do. A component failure or external factor that the pilot could not foresee leads to an inevitable tragic conclusion. But at other times I find myself yelling "Push forward!" or "Go-around!" at the television, to no avail.

However there are also the happy endings, like the TACA Boeing 737 landing on a grassy levee near New Orleans in 1988 or the three double engine failures, involving in total only one person's death, between July 2000 and January 2002. But the best example was when Captain Sullenberger put his Airbus A320 down in the Hudson River after a flock of geese took out both engines in January 2009. I watched that one with great interest, and pride in our profession, and I enjoyed his calm acceptance of the inevitable, and instant decision having examined and discarded all other options. The whole episode played out with total logic.

I followed other cases on an online forum set up by pilots. There was the disappearance of Malaysian 370. How could a large modern airliner like a Boeing 777 just vanish? If it went down where contact was lost then it would have been found quickly. Then the military admitted tracking an unknown radar contact off to the west, and finally a communications company realised that they had received automatic response "pings" from it for many hours after contact was lost. They found a way of tracking the signals very approximately, and decided that the pings ended over the southern Indian Ocean, somewhere west of Australia at about the time fuel would have run out. The question remains: WHY?

Hijackers with political or financial motives seek publicity and issue demands. Otherwise what would be the point? Maybe they failed and crashed, but their organisation would still claim responsibility. Why would a terrorist organisation, or even a lone terrorist, fly the aircraft to the most remote location they could possibly reach? Terrorists go where the news media can find them since that creates terror. But this creates mystery. Besides, a failed hijack or a straightforward accident would have left debris, easily found, like the Air France A330 that stalled and crashed in the Atlantic. That search took several days since a vast area had to be searched, but they found a huge piece of the fin floating, plus bodies and smaller debris.

It is possible that a fire or depressurisation problem made the crew deviate from their programmed route and program a new destination or even select a heading. If the crew later succumbed to smoke or the lack of oxygen, the aircraft would continue on this new programmed route, or the last heading selected, until the fuel ran out and the aircraft crashed. Why no distress call and why has no wreckage turned up after all this time? In any uncontrolled crash the aircraft would be shredded and lots of bits would float, so where are they? At the time of writing (July 2015), not one piece has been identified from Malaysian 370. I know the potential search area is vast, but could there be another possibility?

There are lots of conspiracy theories online but, to me, they all lack credibility. So here is my view, as an airline pilot. I find it very suspicious that the disappearance occurred precisely at the handover point between Malaysia and Vietnam, the first point at which it was out of radio contact. It is too much of a coincidence that the transponder and ACARS both stopped working exactly in the small time-window which is also the perfect point that a pilot would choose to disappear. How could an outsider time a cockpit intrusion to coincide with signing off with Malaysian ATC? Who could time their intervention in the flight to the few seconds between signing off with Malaysian ATC and calling Vietnam? In my view, only the Captain.

Kuala Lumpur Radar called, "Malaysian 370, contact Ho Chi Minh 120.9. Good Night." When the Captain replies "Goodnight, Malaysian 370," to Malaysia but does not check in with Vietnam he can be fairly sure that nobody will notice for some time. Vietnam ATC would eventually notice their non-arrival, call for them on 120.9, check their radar, and call on other frequencies in case they are on another sector by mistake. Then they phone Kuala Lumpur to confirm that the flight left Malaysian airspace, where and when, and what transponder code and contact frequency were given. It slowly and reluctantly dawns on both authorities that the flight is actually missing.

By the time they press the panic button it could be hundreds of miles away, the pilot having made his escape. If nobody but the autopilot was in control the aircraft would have continued on its pre-programmed route to Beijing and beyond, with ACARS and transponder working, until the fuel ran out. But no, the Malaysian Military admitted that their primary radar showed the flight turn around and continue west in Malaysian airspace. My guess is that the military paid little attention and did not perceive it as a threat because the flight originated in their own country. The aircraft made several deliberate looking turns and tracked right along their airspace boundary before heading to the southern Indian ocean so I believe a pilot was in control, with a destination in mind. Which pilot? Time and planning are critical. The Captain can order the co-pilot to leave the cockpit on an errand, but not vice-versa, so in my scenario I have to blame the Captain.

If I were writing the story as credible fiction, I would have the captain sign off with Malaysian ATC with a cheery "Good night, Malaysian 370," and then he spills his coffee down the cockpit side panel and onto his briefcase. He tells the copilot, "Fetch some towels from the toilet for me, and while you are back there order me another coffee. I will check in with Vietnam." Copilots, especially Asian copilots, do not argue with the Captain so he says, "Yes, Sir," and departs immediately.

With the co-pilot gone, the Captain would then lock the cockpit door and select a westerly heading for the autopilot, to steer towards Penang. He pulls the circuit breakers to switch off the radar transponder, the ACARS and even the exterior lights. He puts on his oxygen mask before turning off the air conditioning units and opening the cabin outflow valve to depressurise the cabin. The cabin altitude would climb rapidly from the usual 8000 feet to the aircraft's actual altitude of 35000 feet, or higher, where humans cannot survive for long.

The emergency oxygen for the passengers would last maybe fifteen minutes, the portable bottles used by the cabin crew when moving around (and trying in vain to get into the cockpit) might last half an hour, but after an hour everyone but the Captain would be deeply unconscious, and after two hours all but the Captain would be dead, from hypoxia. The cockpit oxygen supply from cylinders in the equipment bay below is designed to supply four cockpit occupants on pure oxygen in a smoke emergency. For the Captain breathing just supplemental oxygen, on his own this supply would last him for many hours.

On the way to Penang he would slow the aircraft to its most economical cruising speed and program a route for the autopilot to follow from there, around the northern end of Sumatra then south into the Indian ocean. He would program waypoints and a specific final destination in whole degrees at, for example, 28 degrees south 109 degrees east. Then he would settle down for a peaceful night, after the hammering on the cockpit door died away. He could then re-pressurise the cabin and take off his mask. As he approached his final destination position his fuel tanks would be almost empty, and as he programmed the descent into the autopilot he would see the sun begin to light up the eastern sky.

On reaching 1500 feet a few miles short of his 28/109 position fix, he would be relieved to see the early morning sunshine on the expected fishing boat, which would fire off a smoke flare to indicate wind direction. He would perform a visual circuit to position the aircraft for a ditching. As airline pilots are advised to do, by optimistic experts, he would line up the aircraft to touch down on the water near the boat, *along* the swell, as into-wind as possible, and at as low a speed as possible, flaps down, wheels up. Several days passed before the search area switched to the Indian ocean. I'd bet the Captain didn't even realise that the aircraft's ACARS comms equipment would be making an answering ping every hour to that satellite, even when switched off. I didn't.

Could the Captain have somehow done a "Sullenberger" and put the aircraft down on the water intact? Unlikely I think, as the Indian ocean is nowhere near as calm as the Hudson river. The aircraft would likely have broken up to some extent. But just supposing he was lucky and his aircraft floated. Did he go down with it? Or could he possibly have opened the cockpit window and jumped out with his life jacket, and then been picked up by that fishing boat, to watch his aircraft slowly sink towards the ocean floor, more or less intact with all its seat cushions, life jackets and other potential flotsam still on board? My fictional story would end with him sunbathing on an Australian beach with a pina colada, but I cannot possibly explain him killing over two hundred people in between. So, no, I can't believe that is what really happened. It is still a mystery.

(P.S. I had no sooner written the above when a piece of wreckage has been found and identified, from Malaysian 370. But it is not some random piece. It is a piece of wing trailing edge flap that, together with the engines, would be the very first part of the aeroplane to hit the water in a controlled ditching, and the most likely bit to break off and float. To me that strongly suggests a deliberate water landing. So my scenario is still a possibility. Also, wasn't "Sully" a great movie?)

I followed the Germanwings crash in the Alps on the online forum too. It quickly became apparent that the authorities blamed the co-pilot for mass murder, by crashing deliberately after locking the Captain out of the cockpit when he went to the toilet. Many non-pilots chipped into the forum with various ideas about how the Captain should be able to gain entry to the cockpit in these circumstances using a secret key or password. But they are missing the point.

If the Captain knew a secret way to get back in then terrorists could get it out of him. This secure cockpit arrangement was set up in the aftermath of 9/11 to make it possible to isolate the cockpit. The idea was that terrorists in the cabin could not get at the pilots or even talk to them, or threaten them. It is true that at any time the terrorists could still bring down the aircraft, but they cannot possibly use it as a guided incendiary missile as in 9/11 if the pilots ignore them and land the aircraft at an airfield where friendly soldiers are ready to surround it. The problem with the locked cockpit door turned out to be that there is nothing that anyone behind it can do if the person in front is hell bent on suicide.

One solution might be to have the toilet door in the cockpit, and the locked door behind that. The pilots would get their own private loo and the passengers must go elsewhere. That is still not fool-proof though. While the suicidal pilot's first choice might be to do it in privacy, his second option might be to incapacitate or simply overpower the other pilot and I do not think that there is a solution. A determined and strong pilot with suicide and murder in mind will always have the capability to crash his aircraft. Fortunately such pilots are exceedingly rare. If they still exist, they must be kept out of the cockpit.

Another solution would be to turn the clock back forty years and revert to a three-crew cockpit, like we had on the Trident and L1011 Tristar. A single suicidal person in the cockpit could be kept in check by one crew member while the other controls the aeroplane until the cabin crew can intervene, as you can read below. It should work, but the industry could not cope with a 50% increase in pilot requirements. The official solution, and all that can realistically be done, is to ensure that a cabin crew member is present in the cockpit during toilet breaks.

On 29 December 2000, shortly before 9/11, aircraft still operated with the door to the cockpit closed, but not locked, as cabin crew came back and forth with drinks, meals and cabin reports. There was often a toilet at the front of the cabin and very occasionally a passenger opened the cockpit door in mistake for the toilet, then stumbled back out mumbling apologies.

But on that day on a BA flight to Nairobi, a mentally disturbed passenger entered the cockpit when the co-pilot was at the controls and the Captain and spare co-pilot were out of their seats (rest bunk and toilet). The passenger attacked the co-pilot and tried to crash the aeroplane. He was a big strong man and the co-pilot was trying to fend him off as well as save the aeroplane. The Boeing 747-400 stalled twice and banked until wings were vertical during the struggle.

The Captain intervened, engaging the passenger from behind. By gouging both thumbs into his eye sockets and pulling hard he managed to get the man away from the controls allowing the co-pilot to regain control, then with help from his other co-pilot he dragged him from the cockpit. Then the cabin crew and other passengers helped overpower and subdue the madman. What heroes those pilots were that day! The aircraft was scrapped.

Could I have done that (the eye gouging)? I have often wondered; it would take some nerve. But, given the alternative, I think that I could, and would. I think any of us would in those circumstances: each pilot has to be that sort of person, including the women.

STOP PRESS COVID-19 update

Much has changed for pilots since my day. Now pilots usually have to pay their own training with a bank loan or family reserves. Pilots work more hours with less time off in foreign hotels, cheaper hotels than we used, instead of crew meals they bring sandwiches, and pension benefits are much reduced. But the COVID pandemic has caused chaos in the industry. Airlines have shed old aircraft, cancelled orders for new ones, thrown thousands of pilots out of work and slashed the salaries of others. It's far worse than the oil crisis, the terror attacks, the financial crash or anything else in my experience.

Here's an idea though! Bring back the three-pilot cockpit. The seat is there already. Here is a unique opportunity to solve the security problems of 2-crew aircraft now that plenty of pilots are available. No pilot need be left alone again. For critical flight phases there will always be three pilots on duty, eliminating half of the historical accidents, like BM at Kegworth, the Germanwings death dive, Malaysian disappearance, and many others. We shall see if Airlines, and Government regulating authorities, care more about safety measures than profit. Does anybody really believe that safety comes first?

Chapter 12
Aircraft Designer

In Chapter one I skated over my University training to be an aircraft designer. Well, now that's all I am. While flying Tristar I wrote the book Basic Aeronautics for Modellers,[3] then I shelved it for Highland Division. Then in 1995 I had it published and started writing in model magazines. But since I retired from that in 2011 I have been only a full-time aircraft designer, and builder, test pilot, development pilot, service pilot and airshow pilot.

From the age of ten I have been interested in model aeroplanes, and have flown a great many, starting from kits normally, or published plans or second-hand airframes occasionally. I also bought some of the new pre-built models when they became available, but nothing compares to the thrill of design. When you land a model after an exciting display, and people remark (as they do), "That flies really well! Where did you get it?"

It is so satisfying to say, "I started with a clean sheet of paper, drew it out and then built it myself." You don't get that with a kit, or a ready-made from Toys'R'Us.

Often, design starts from a commercial kit and the thought, "I can do better than that." Many model builders do just that. It is not so difficult to take an existing design and change a few unimportant shapes to achieve something that looks different but is essentially the same as the original. If you keep the wing section, and make the tail the same area and distance back, it will fly in a similar manner even with a re-drawn fuselage and fin. That is a good starting point if you want to do your own thing. Reading my 'Basic Aeronautics' book should

---

[3] My first book, Basic Aeronautics for Modellers, is still available from Waterstones, Amazon or Sarik Hobbies. www.sarikhobbies.com

give any model builder the knowledge of what details matter, and what they can personalise. I just go one step further back.

I have never designed my own aerofoil sections, for example. There are thousands to choose from, with graphs in books showing how they perform, so I have done some reading and chosen my favourites. Each section is good for its own specific use. I choose the Clark Y for easy to build trainer or sporty models, a symmetrical NACA for aerobatic models that have to fly upside down some of the time, or strangely curved Selig sections for specialised heavy-lift planes.

I always draw the wing first. The wing section is determined by the aircraft's purpose in life. Then I draw a tailplane, sized and shaped to enable it to keep the wing under control. That usually means a thin symmetrical section a few wing chords behind the wing. The combination of a wing and a tail demands that the Centre of Gravity must be within a certain small range. I am used to that from commercial flying wherein the Centre of Gravity is calculated and adjusted with precision before each successful flight. The same goes for models. Get the CG wrong and the maiden flight can be brief.

With the required Centre of Gravity marked on the paper, the designer can draw a fuselage around the parts. It has to keep all the parts together, and look nice. Well, looking nice is a bonus, and beauty is in the eye of the beholder. All my designs look nice to me, which is what matters. Above all the design has to be practical to build, to fly and to maintain. Some of my own designs are still flying after ten years and I do not tire of them the way I do with ready-mades.

My first design from scratch was an aerobatic model. I had built an aerobat from a kit, but it crashed due to a design fault. I rebuilt it, fixed the fault and flew it for a while but I knew I could do better. I started with my big sheet of paper, pencils, erasers, set squares and so on. I started with the wing section at the wing root, using a section developed by NACA in the USA at 15% thickness. For the wingtip I used a different NACA symmetrical section but only 12% thick, and I blended the two shapes together along the length of the wing. I made the leading edge straight and swept the trailing edge forward to give a sensible amount of taper, and gave the wing slight positive incidence.

Then I drew the tailplane, a similar shape in planform and with a thin symmetrical section. I marked the Centre of Gravity that I calculated. The fin was drawn in above the tailplane using a shape and size that just looked normal. I drew the engine a bit ahead of the wing, then moved it a bit further ahead to achieve a better balance around my chosen Centre of Gravity. When I finished, my pencils and rubber were noticeably smaller, but my creation looked good.

Once built it flew very well too, on a tricycle undercarriage (with a nosewheel), and that was just the mark 1. The model flew so well that I knew it was worth developing further, but I needed a name, and that is often the hardest part. Every time I came up with a suitable name it had been used somewhere at some time by someone else. Maybe I am not very original. But the model was such a joy to fly that I settled on a Gaelic word *Sonas* which means joy or happiness. Perfect, and I'm confident it has never been used before.

The mark 2 had a stiffer rear fuselage and a quarter inch more dihedral. The mark 3 was much smaller, the mark 4 was enormous with a 74cc petrol engine (and a tailwheel). For the mark 5 I designed floats to operate from water, and the latest one is an in-between size, and also acquired a set of floats. When a model works that well I like to make larger and smaller versions.

The same thing happened when I designed a hull-in-water flying boat with wingtip floats. It performed very well, and so I made a smaller one with two electric motors, then a bigger version with one engine, and another bigger still. All but the first were named after fresh-water Scottish lochs and had many changes over the years. The biggest of these (so far) is called Lomond, which has two 4 to 6 c.c. Engines. Twin engined models are rare, as most modellers worry that when one engine stops the model will crash out of control.

We have all seen it happen. But I used to look forward to the occasional engine failure as it gave me the chance to use the full-size engine failure techniques, so often practised but never used. They worked splendidly on my models. I could fly a single engined approach on Lomond and go-around (overshoot) from just a foot or two above the water and climb safely away for another circuit.

My post-retirement design adventure has been sport jets. That is, a radio-controlled model powered by a miniature gas turbine engine, but designed from scratch, not a scale model of a full-size aeroplane. I designed mine to be as simple as possible to build, and as easy to fly as my fast aerobatic models. I wanted to have the absolute minimum of maintenance and the ability to fly from virtually any model airfield.

Many scale jet aircraft need to fly from tarmac runways and that limits their use, because their retracting undercarriage has wheels too small and mechanism too delicate to use on bumpy grass. However all model jets really do need flaps.

It is essential to increase the drag for the landing approach as the engines have significant thrust even at idle. Flaps are one complication jets cannot do without.

My most successful design was conceived as a jet trainer, by which I mean a model that would make an ideal introduction to model gas turbines for someone already proficient in flying aerobatic models. It has a fixed (not retracting) undercarriage of great strength, large 100 mm diameter main wheels and the engine is both fully exposed for maintenance, and neatly tucked away so that you need to look for it. The construction is all quite familiar for the experienced aeromodeller and its performance is stunning.

I have flown it at several model airshows in Britain. The model is called JT (for jet trainer) normally written as ***JayTee***. For a time I fitted an electronic device that measured and recorded airspeed, groundspeed (from GPS), height above the runway, heading and a couple of other parameters. The airspeed measured in level flight was about 125 mph, landing speed was 25 mph and the diameter of the loops was amazing. I found that when I pulled tight loops I was stressing the airframe to plus and minus nine 'g.'

As a step onward from that I designed a pair of floats, and built a second complete aeroplane. The floats were fitted to the original model, and it was flown at many waterplane venues in Scotland, and in the Lake District. The floats suited the model very well allowing easy take-offs and good touchdowns as long as the flare was prolonged so that the tails of the floats touched first. A touchdown too soon led to a skip, and a second touchdown, even a third. Because there is no airflow over the tail surfaces while taxiing, a water rudder at the rear of one of the floats was needed.

A second airframe was fitted with the wheeled undercarriage and the latest model of the jet engine, whose thrust had increased from 6kg to 8kg. The thrust/weight ratio was now 1:1 even at take-off weight and now the two-litre fuel tank lasted only six minutes. The name of the original shoulder winged model remains JayTee.

The next step forward was an even faster version with a smaller wingspan and a low mounted wing, and I called it JayLow. I am still not great with names. This one sports an RAF Trainer colour scheme that does suit it very well. It is important for this kind of model to have a colour scheme that stands out well at a distance and makes it easy to see the model's orientation.

It is often the way that life goes around in circles, and so it has been with my relationship to aircraft. As a young lad I saw drawings in my father's office of an aircraft that I would eventually fly in British Airways. And my very latest design has brought me back there again.

For many years I dreamed of having a large jet powered model of the Trident airliner. I discussed it with friends, I photographed the example in the Museum at Duxford, I read magazine articles about it, and dreamed, for years. Eventually however I had to admit there was no easy way. I admitted to the experts that I had too little knowledge of things like wing sections and construction, details like how the undercarriage worked, how the flaps moved and so on. The wing was especially complex, with a change of section, taper and everything else, a third of the way out and sharply angled away from the centreline.

But I had an idea of how it might be modelled, with an inner panel of balsa-sheeted foam, cut with a hot wire to blend a symmetrical root to a cambered join section, with that awkward angle. That would mate with a relatively simple outer panel using balsa ribs, spars and sheeting, with a little washout. I decided I had to prove it by making one, to a small scale, a twentieth of the full size Trident 2E. It actually looked quite realistic.

Alright, I thought, now build a left wing, add a rudimentary fuselage and tail and see if it might actually fly. I wanted to keep it simple, fixed undercarriage, no flaps, one engine (the middle one), just to prove that a scale flying model, more than twice this size, was feasible. Of course ambition carried me away, I bought a tiny turbine engine, smaller than a coke can, I hot wire cut a cylinder of foam for the fuselage, carved a foam nose and built up a balsa tail section and painted it to resemble the one at Duxford. Behind the nose windows I fitted a little pilot.

With great trepidation I fired up my tiny turbine, which roared and smelled just like the real thing, I opened the throttle and off it went, leaping into the air and flying really well. My Trident could loop, roll, and even fly inverted but not deep stall, unlike the real thing. The only thing it would not do is land, it just kept flying and flying. I had to shut down the engine to get it back on the runway. After several similar attempts I gave in and added flaps, and that added enough drag to achieve a landing with the engine running.

I still have not started on the much bigger version, but maybe one day I shall. Meantime I have more to learn from the little one. The thrill of flying something that I designed and built from scratch will never fade.

The End

Glossary

9/11	The terrorist attack on the twin towers of the World Trade Centre in New York on 11 September 2001, that changed everything.
ACARS	air/ground data transfer system, via satellite. Includes cockpit printer.
Aileron	The waggly bit on the back of the wing out at the end, that banks the aeroplane.
Apron	The parking area for aircraft which may be around the terminal, or a bus-ride away.
Alternate	An airport not too far from the planned destination that has forecast good weather.
Approach	The bit of the flight from the last beacon on the route to the runway.
APU	Auxiliary Power Unit. A small additional turbine engine that supplies air conditioning and electric power when parked.
ASI	Air Speed Indicator, reading in knots, occasionally mph on US airplanes.
ATC	Air Traffic Control
ATIS	At busy airports the latest weather report is broadcast continually on its own frequency to save the ATC controller repeating himself to every aircraft.
Autothrottle	Like cruise control on a car, it adjusts engine power to try to maintain a selected airspeed.
BA	British Airways
BCal	British Caledonian Airways
BEA	British European Airways
BOAC	British Overseas Airways Corporation
CAT	Clear Air Turbulence. Ruffled air that's not in clouds.
CDG	Code for Charles de Gaulle, main airport of Paris

CSD	On wide bodied aircraft in BA the chief cabin steward was given the title of Cabin Service Director.
Daytrip	A trip departing base, landing at destination, and returning the same day.
Downwind	In the same direction as the wind. Flying parallel to the runway a mile or so away, in the opposite direction to the landing and take-off traffic.
EBB	Three letter code for Entebbe airport, Uganda.
EFIS	Electronic Flight Instrument System, aka, glass cockpit.
ETA	Estimated Time of Arrival.
ETOPS	Extended range Twin OPerationS.
Final	The last bit of the approach, lined up with the runway.
FMC	Flight Management Computer. It is programmed before the flight with the route, weight and fuel details and can control the whole flight through the autopilot.
Glass cockpit	A colloquial expression for electronic instruments displayed on screens.
Go-around	If the pilot decides not to land, but opens the throttles on final approach to climb away instead, that's a go-around in US English, or an overshoot to old British flying chaps.
Golden Rivet	There was a myth going round, adopted from naval folklore, that every aircraft had, somewhere, a single rivet made from gold.
Headwind	If the wind is coming from wherever the plane is flying towards, it has a headwind, which does not affect how it flies but will delay its arrival. A very strong headwind can even blow an aircraft backwards relative to the ground without the pilot knowing, and without showing on instruments.
ILS	Instrument Landing System. A precise 3-D radio beam that the pilot or autopilot can follow, to (and along) the runway
JFK	Three letter code for New York's John F Kennedy airport
Latitude (lat)	How far up (or down) the world you are in degrees, from zero at the equator to ninety degrees North or South at the poles.
LHR	Three letter code for London Heathrow airport
loadsheet	Document showing the total weight, load distribution, and aircraft balance.
Longitude (long)	How far round the world you are in degrees, from zero in Greenwich (London) to 180 degrees East or West (same place) round the other side.

NDB	Non-Directional Beacon. Badly named radio beacon that transmits the same signal all over (omni-directional).
Nightstop	A work trip in which you fly off to destination, spend a night in the hotel, and fly back to base next day.
Operations (or just Ops)	The nerve centre of an airline, where people constantly make decisions about what happens to aeroplanes, crews and passengers.
Overshoot	In UK English it is an aborted landing, or go-around, power up and climb away instead of landing. In American it is running off the end of the runway.
PAR	Precision Approach Radar. A controller takes one aeroplane at a time and, by watching it on his very accurate 3-D radar, gives the pilot constant guidance instructions towards his runway. Labour intensive.
RAF	Royal Air Force, the fly-boys of the Queen in the UK.
Roller	A Rolls Royce aero engine. (or transport home from work?)
Roller	A landing, followed immediately by reconfiguration (take-off flap), and then opening the throttles for a take-off on the remaining runway, for practice.
Rudder	The bit at the back of the aeroplane that waggles sideways, connected to the pilot's feet.
Sector	A flight that includes a start-up, take-off, fly somewhere, landing and shutdown.
Secondary radar (SSR)	The aircraft's transponder broadcasts a coded signal giving ident, altitude, position etc in response to a ground station's 'who's out there?' signal.
Speedbird	The callsign of all BOAC and BA flights (followed by flight number)
Standover	A whole day off away somewhere, that does not include a flying duty.
Tailwind	If the wind is blowing over the ground from a direction right behind the aircraft in flight, it has a tailwind. Its speed over the ground is its airspeed added to the wind speed.
Taxiway	A roadway for aircraft, connecting parking areas to the runways and hangars. Each section is numbered to enable ATC to give route instructions, and for pilots to report their position. At large airports, taxiways have centreline and edge lights, and cross-bars (stop-bars) used like traffic lights.

TCAS	Traffic Collision Avoidance System. Each aircraft with a transponder broadcasts position, track and height information, listens for other aircraft, and the TCAS computer calculates possible collisions and warns the pilots.
Toe-brakes	A hinged extension added upwards to each side of the rudder-bar. Pressing forward and down with your toes applies the wheelbrake on that side.
Touch-and-go	Another expression for a Roller landing (above).
Turnaround	The time between parking at the end of one flight and starting up for the next flight (back to base usually).
Walkaround	Sometimes walkround. The external check on an aeroplane before flight for which the pilot walks all the way around the aircraft checking everything in general, and all specified items, for damage.

Printed in Great Britain
by Amazon